KENNETH NOLAND

Karen Wilkin

KENNETH NOLAND

RIZZOLI
NEW YORK

Acknowledgements:

My thanks to Dorothy Cater and the staff at Galeria Joan
Prats, and to Jim Bird, without whom this project would
never have been realized. I am indebted to Mignette
Hollyman for her patience and assistance, and to Carolina
Kroon for her perceptiveness and helpfulness. Finally, I am
deeply grateful to Kenneth Noland for being so generous
with his time and for making this project so stimulating and
enriching an experience.

All quotations from Kenneth Noland from conversations with
the author 1986-1988.

Jacket:
Doors: Yellow Fin. 1989.
Acrylic on canvas, 37 × 40⅞ in. (94 × 100 cm).
Collection of the artist.
Courtesy Salander-O'Reilly Galleries, New York.
Photo: Steven Sloman.

First published in the United States of America in 1990 by
RIZZOLI INTERNATIONAL PUBLICATIONS, INC.
300 Park Avenue South, New York, NY 10010

© 1990 Ediciones Polígrafa, S. A.

© Text Karen Wilkin

Library of Congress Cataloging-in-Publication Data

Wilkin, Karen.
    Kenneth Noland/Karen Wilkin.
        p.   cm.
    Includes bibliographical references.
    ISBN 0-8478-1240-5
    1. Noland. Kenneth, 1924-   . 2. Artists—United States—Biograpy.
I. Title.
N6537.N65W55 1990
760'.092—dc20   90-52614
                                                      CIP

Color separation by Reprocolor Llovet, S. A., Barcelona
Printed and bound by La Polígrafa, S. A.
Parets del Vallès (Barcelona)
Dep. Leg. B. 33.424 - 1990 (Printed in Spain)

CONTENTS

Introduction
7

Chronology
25

Selected Bibliography
26

Major Museum Collections
27

Illustrations
29

List of Illustrations
126

Kenneth Noland, South Salem, NY, April 1982. Photo: Harvey Stein.

I

To say "Kenneth Noland" is to call up a modern day icon. Whether the image that comes to mind is one of his celebrated "Circles," "Chevrons" or "Stripes," one of his less familiar series known as "Cat's Eyes" or "Plaids," or one of his extraordinary shaped canvases, Noland's name stands for a particular kind of American painting — one based on the potency of color. His pictures are among the most original, elegant and unabashedly beautiful of our time. And they are among the most abstract, admired as much because they test the limits of what can be eliminated (without compromising reason or expression) as for their seductive hues. In Noland's hands, the orchestration and placement of colors have become, almost for the first time in the history of Western art, independently expressive elements, removed from even the most tenuous connection with any preexisting image. The powerful associative qualities of color harmonies, like evocative sounds or scents, are made the carriers of profound emotions, but they are completely detached from any specific reference, from anecdote or symbol.

Curiously, despite the fame of these pictures, they represent only a portion of Noland's work. After more than thirty years of serious, inventive painting, the first two decades of his career remain the best documented and consequently the most familiar. His retrospective exhibition, organized by the Guggenheim Museum and circulated in the United States in 1977, focused on this period, beginning with the "Circles" and ending — of necessity — with the first series of shaped canvases, painted in 1976. The major monograph on the artist, published by Abrams, New York, also appeared in 1977. Then, too, Noland's art has been ineluctably associated with the 1960s and 70s. His paintings can be seen as paradigms of their period, images that define the best abstract painting of the time, so much so that Noland is sometimes presented as though his importance were determined chiefly by his first twenty years of mature work, as though he had ceased making art at the end of the 1970s.

Nothing could be less accurate. Noland, like any artist worth serious attention, has continued to grow and change, making some of his most daring ventures into new territory in the past ten years, building on his past, extending his reach, and intensifying the emotional climate of his work. Noland has returned to old obsessions, but with a difference; he has more fully explored the possibilities of shaping canvases, reexamined the "Chevron" format in fresh and surprising ways, investigated new media. The exquisite sensibility and sensitivity to color that we associate with him are still present, but there is a new robustness and physicality to his work, a new emphasis on shape and surface. Most recently, he has produced a group of remarkable constructed paintings that both sum up and challenge his preoccupations of the past three decades.

The "Circles" of the late '50s are the first unequivocal statements of Noland's persistent themes and can be reasonably said to signal the beginning of his maturity as an artist. When he made them, he was thirty-three and had been painting seriously for more than ten years. At twenty-two, after serving in the U.S. Air Force from 1942 to 1946, he used his G. I. Bill benefits to study painting and music at Black Mountain College and in Paris. Black Mountain was near Noland's home town, Asheville, North Carolina, but more important, it was a vibrant center of the avant-garde in the arts. There, Noland studied briefly with the head of the Art Department, Josef Albers, assimilating his Bauhaus-derived color theory, and with Ilya Bolotowsky, who introduced him to modernist geometry, particularly to Mondrian. Noland studied, too, with John Cage and met other faculty members — innovators such as Merce Cunningham, Buckminster Fuller, and Willem and Elaine de Kooning.

In the fall of 1948, Noland went to Paris to study with the sculptor Ossip Zadkine. Painting, however, was his dominant concern and his first one-man exhibition, held at Galerie Raymond Creuze in the spring of 1949, was of works he had painted in Paris. The following fall, a student-teaching grant brought Noland back to the United States, to Washington D.C., where he settled. He returned to Black Mountain for a summer session in 1950, where he met Clement Greenberg, the most perceptive critic and spokesman for the advanced art of the period. Noland's friendship with Helen Frankenthaler dates from her visit to Black Mountain College that summer, as well. He visited Greenberg frequently in New York, in the coming years, and through him, met, among others, Anthony Caro, when the British sculptor visited America for the first time. (Seeing Noland's paintings on that trip helped to provoke Caro's subsequent shift to abstraction.) Noland met David Smith in these early years, through his future wife Cornelia Langer, who had been a student of Smith's. The connection became even closer when Smith married a school friend of Ms. Langer's. Noland's friendship with Smith endured until the sculptor's death in 1965. They saw each other regularly in New York, often with their friends and colleagues Helen Frankenthaler and Robert Motherwell. Later, in 1963, Noland moved to Vermont, within relatively easy visiting distance of Smith's home in upstate New York. A tantalizing image emerges of these four luminaries of American abstraction, frequenting each other's studios, scrutinizing each other's work. By 1964, Jules Olitski and Anthony Caro were teaching at Bennington College, near where Noland lived, and the exchanges became even richer.

One of Noland's most significant friendships, with the painter Morris Louis, was one of his oldest. They met in 1952, when they taught at the same Washington art school, and began a dialogue that lasted until Louis's death in 1962. For these two ambitious young artists, relatively isolated in Washington and struggling with notions of excellence and risk in painting, this exchange was invaluable. In 1953, Noland and Louis travelled to New York to visit galleries and studios. Noland introduced Louis to Greenberg, who arranged for them to see the new work of the young and virtually unknown Frankenthaler. The now famous encounter proved decisive. Louis, in fact, later described Frankenthaler as "the bridge between Pollock and what was possible." Her large scale paintings, made by staining thin color into raw canvas, suggested a way of working that used Pollock as a point of departure, rather than a model, a way of translating the all-overness and elusive visual qualities of Pollock's skeins of paint into a new kind of disembodied color painting.

Pollock, and Abstract Expressionism, in general, had already pointed towards a direction that Noland found provocative. "Until Abstract Expressionism," he says, "you had to have something to paint *about*, some kind of subject matter. Even though Kandinsky and Arthur Dove were improvising earlier, it didn't take. They had to have symbols, suggested natural images or geometry, which was something *real* structurally. That gave them something to paint about. What was new was the idea that something you looked at could be like something you heard." For Noland, who is as knowledgeable about music as he is about painting, the notion was irresistible.

Back in Washington, Louis and Noland began to experiment with the stain technique. Louis eventually devised a way of layering and "veiling," with broad pours of color. Noland tried a number of formats, but before long a concentric layout began to preoccupy him, taking various forms until it resolved itself as a series of clear bands generated by the acknowledgement of the center of a square canvas. "I knew what a circle could do," Noland says. "Both eyes focus on it. It stamps itself out, like a dot. This, in turn, causes one's vision to spread, as in a mandala in Tantric art." This deceptively simple composition allowed Noland to concentrate on color, but it also demanded that he pay attention to the smallest nuances of edge, density and placement; how wide a band was, how thickly or thinly painted, how far it was from other bands, how far from the center or perimeter of the canvas were all as crucial as its hue. Color seems to dominate in these pictures yet it is impossible to separate color from structure, since one seems to determine the other. "People talk about color in the 'Circles,' but they are also about scales and juxtapositions," Noland says about them today. "Making them taught me everything about scale."

The "Circles" proved seminal and set the pattern for much of Noland's future practice. He has remained faithful, for example, to the notion of working in series, evidence of both his inventiveness and his thrift. By stabilizing a few compositional "givens," he can extract the last conceivable possibility from a fruitful idea and, since he does not have to invent structure for each new painting, he can instead concentrate on other, perhaps more subtle, issues. Noland still appears to enjoy treading the narrow boundary between the freedom this way of working engenders and its simultaneous discipline. Yet this clearheaded method and Noland's insistence on presenting his work in coherent groups suggests a degree of systematicness and programmaticness that is, in fact, belied by his improvisatory approach to working and his wholehearted reliance upon informed intuition. Even his use of repeated formats is arguably a way of courting the unexpected, since the shared layout of a series both accentuates and cancels similarity. The very likeness between the ''Circle'' pictures, for example, makes differences between them even more telling, both for the viewer and their maker.

Noland believes firmly in the necessity of remaining alert to suggestions that arise in the course of working and of responding to those suggestions. ''I believe in working every day,'' he says, ''and not necessarily repeating one way of working. I like to make something come out of trial and error methods — fooling around with mediums and taking the chance of its not coming to anything.'' Noland has said, not altogether facetiously, that ''at least 80% of art is getting control over your materials'' and, more seriously, ''Artists are mechanics who work with their hands, make things. Artists are involved with the *means* of creativity, the nature of skills, the revelation of making. Art comes from the work, I see a painting as an expressive entity. There's no picture that I know of where the subject carries as much expressive possibility as the actual execution of the picture.''

He traces some of these attitudes to his Asheville childhood. His father was an amateur painter, his mother an amateur musician, so the fine arts were part of his everyday life; but beyond that, he describes a particular attitude toward craft, toward the creation of even ordinary objects, that he associates with his home town. ''One of my grandfathers was a blacksmith,'' he says, ''and all the plumbers and carpenters and electricians, people who did things with their hands, thought of themselves as artists because they were good at doing things. They were proud of their making skills.''

Noland credits David Smith with having had an even more profound effect on how he works and how he thinks about making art. Smith's workman-like habits and his ''factory-studio'' with its vast stockpiles of material, set a standard for perceptive artists of Noland's generation. Smith believed that keeping regular working hours and having abundant material freed the artist; it kept him from becoming precious and allowed him to work without inhibition. Noland explains, ''When I first met David, I didn't know how to set myself up so that I *could* work. In those days, you'd buy a paintbox and an easel, take a couple of canvases, work on them and then put the paints away and fold up the easel. That was the basic way of trying to be a painter while you did other things, like having jobs to support yourself. David advised 'Buy materials when you can and in quantity. Don't just get one stretcher or one tube of paint. It's more practical to accumulate as much money as you can and buy as much canvas and paint as you can'.''

For Noland, over the years, and particularly in the last decade, his belief that ''art comes from the work'' has led him to explore as wide a range of materials and methods as of images. In addition to painting, he has made clay pieces, cast-paper works and monotypes, collaborated on a monumental architectural mural, worked with Native American Navajo weavers, and experimented with computer and video art. He is also an inventive sculptor. Noland feels that each foray into new territory informs the rest of his art. It helps to release his intuition and keeps him from relying on the known and familiar. His receptiveness to new notions, derived from the experience of working, whatever the medium, has, in fact, led to a body of work far more erratic and eccentric than the rationally ordered series presented to the public. Along the way, there have been what Noland calls his ''odd-ball'' pictures, often radically different from anything we associate easily with his work, some abandoned, some stored mentally for future use. ''I have to work things out by painting them,'' Noland says. ''I can't just imagine what will happen. I have to do it and see it. That's the only way I find out if it will go anywhere.''

Yet continuity has been a hallmark of Noland's work since the beginning. Each new series has been a logical development of his past concerns, at the same time that it proposed new notions. Shared characteristics have often seemed as striking as differences. This is not to say that Noland's pictures have suffered from sameness. Far from it. (Obviously, when they do not seem freshly conceived, they fail, and Noland usually knows it.) Rather, the things we have come to expect of him, since those first, unforgettable "Circles," have always, happily, been present: a quickly perceived, frontal structure that fused color, shape and dimension into an instantaneous whole, along with unpredictable color and immaculate surfaces. The most evident changes were more often than not changes in layout, which, in turn, provoked (or resulted from) alterations in color and scale. "I had to find a way in each picture to change the drawing, shaping and tactile qualities to make these elements expressive," Noland says, "as the color had subsumed the possibility of these parts being on an equal basis of expressiveness." The "Circles," for example, began as declarations of symmetry. Assemblies of rather loose, broad bands of color proceeded from the center of the canvas, determining by their density and sequence the eventual size of the square on which they were painted. Later in the series, this sense of measurement and interval was heightened by Noland's translation of the brushy bands of the first "Circles" into tense, widely spaced, clean-edged, narrow rings; the larger expanses of pale, raw canvas in these "hard-edge" "Circles," made color seem more concentrated and often, more brilliant and dense than in the earlier pictures. These crisp "Circles" were followed by the "Cat's Eyes," which can be described as irregular, uncentered and, above all, visually saturated versions of their predecessors. In some, the figure, as if in defiance of the density of the paint and color that surround it, floats free of the center of the painting, seemingly positioned on the canvas only by pressures exerted by the two vertical edges. As in the "Circles," the edges seem to repel the centralized rings of color, whose natural tendency is to expand outward.

In the "Chevrons," which followed, Noland diagrammed the forces of his preceding series, literally connecting the center of the painting to its edges with a series of V-shaped bars of color. In the largest of these, the V reaches generously from corner to corner, like arms outstretched; in smaller paintings, the gesture is more discreet, more compressed, but in both types, the symmetry of the "Chevron" is precise. Later, Noland allowed the point of the "Chevron" to drift away from the center in a surprisingly loose-jointed and playful variation on the motif, but eventually, symmetry and orderliness dominated. In these "Chevrons" — tip-tilted squares where the canvas is framed, embraced or filled with L-shaped color bars — geometry usurps the entire painting. These L-shaped bars then gave way to stacked diagonals that form elongated "Diamonds" whose compressed shapes inevitably suggest a squarer diamond seen in perspective. In some of these pictures, Noland teases us with this implication, shifting the color bands from light to dark in a kind of abstract version of aerial perspective, but ultimately he subverts illusionism by the way he puts color together, just as he had subverted the potentially static, emblematic imagery of the "Circles" by the way he varied color, widths and placement.

Noland found that he could eliminate the relative complexity of the "Chevrons" and "Diamonds" in his next series, the horizontal "Stripes" of the late '60s. In these, perhaps more than in any of Noland's pictures at the time, image and means are inextricably fused. The length of the stripes determines one dimension of the painting, while the number of stripes, their widths and intervals, determines the other. Both dimensions are crucial. Noland often seems to question the limits of seeability; the width of a long horizontal picture decides how far away the viewer positions himself — how far back must you stand to see the whole canvas? — and that, in turn, affects how the delicately adjusted stacks of colored stripes are seen. Are the differences between hues and between paint and raw canvas readily apparent? Or do they function like visual chords? At the same time, the "Stripes" draw you towards them to perceive the nuances of color bars and their spacing. Noland is acutely aware of how these pictures affect the spectator: "I believe that there are varying points of contact. You have to be able to see the whole thing first. All great paintings are sculptures — there's so much of the *actualness* about it that a great painting forces you into a visual, physical movement of yourself. That's what determines the way you experience a painting kinetically. You move closer, you sight down it, you tilt your head, you step back, you feel as though you are in it. That being *in it* is just as important as looking from a distance."

Noland spent years exploring the implications of the "Stripes," inventing seemingly endless variations, from complex orchestrations of multiple stripes to "empty" centers with concentrated groupings at top and bottom. (The latter were painted at about the same time that Noland's colleague, Jules Olitski, was emptying out the centers of his paintings and emphasizing their edges with linear drawing.)

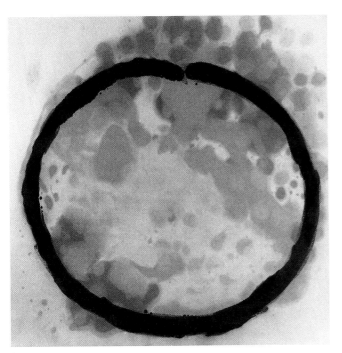

Globe. 1956.
Magna on canvas, 60×60 in. (154.4×152.4 cm).
Cornelia Noland Reis Collection.

Advert. 1963.
Acrilic on canvas, 47×47 in. (119.4×119.4 cm).
Dartmouth College Museum and Galleries, Hanover, N.H.

The stacking of bands in the "Stripes," for all the horizontality of the motif, was, in fact, a stimulus to verticality, a notion that Noland explored in his next series, the "Plaids" of the mid-1970s. Characteristically, he was not content merely to turn a horizontal picture upright, but forced himself to rethink his approach to structure. In all of his earlier series, he had carefully avoided overlapping any elements; bars of color were placed parallel, so that whether their edges touched or were separated by raw canvas became extremely important. But in the "Plaids," overlapping is a primary theme. The vertical fields are dissected by slender grids and the places where bars overlap are emphasized by aggressive changes in color and density.

"These pictures owe something to Mondrian," but more by affinity than by direct example. Mondrian's paintings, for all their radical abstractness, still adhere to a traditional notion of color as a means of identifying separate elements. His "pure" primaries, his reds, blues and yellows, are adjuncts to the basic black and white skeleton of his pictures, so that color never assumes quite the structural, generating role it plays in Noland's paintings. Then, too, Mondrian's grids, his harmonious vertical-horizontal relationships, impersonal surfaces and emptied-out images, like his economical color, are metaphors for a state of ideal order. Noland's "Plaids," like the rest of his paintings, are in one sense, literal; they are not equivalents for anything else, but self-sufficient, eloquent objects.

The "Plaids," while predominantly vertical, also included several square diamonds and tondos. Noland seemed fascinated by the tensions and harmonies he could set up between a declaratively shaped canvas and the nodal concentrations of intersecting color bars. Even when the grid was more or less evenly distributed across the shape, he stressed the intersections, emphasizing the points of greatest interruption of the "supporting" shape. Given these preoccupations, Noland's next series, the shaped canvases of 1976, seems inevitable.

The shapes, over the next few years, ranged from relatively regular near-rectangles, slightly irregular due to the subtle warpings of their edges and slicing of their corners, to eccentric irregular hexagons and unnameable, slender figures sometimes referred to as "Surfboards." It comes as no surprise to learn that Noland has made sculpture that employs planes of steel closely related to the shapes of his canvases. One discipline obviously nourishes the other. In some of his shaped canvases, Noland at once emphasized and distorted the edges of his shapes by means of color changes and groupings of color bands, while in others, fans of color cut across the shape at unexpected angles. In still others, he abandoned chromatic color in favor of an astonishingly subtle range of blacks, greys, near-

Kenneth Noland at the Experimental Workshop, San Francisco.

blacks and creamy whites and yellows. (Perceived at first as a retreat from his gifts as a colorist, these austere canvases have proved over time to be some of the strongest of the shaped series.) No matter what Noland's specific approach, in these paintings, the effect is to alter our perception of tangible shape because of his placement of intangible color.

Throughout all of these variations and permutations, Noland's paintings have depended upon compositions as lucid in their structural logic as the facade of any classical temple. It is perfectly obvious that the vertical columns of the Parthenon stand on the podium and, in turn, support the architrave, frieze and pediment, and equally obvious that a subtle relationship of size and proportions governs the whole; a similar clarity and a similar sense of increment is obtained in Noland's paintings. One elegantly adjusted unit has been added to another and another and another, to make a single, apparently rational, whole. But for all their seeming straightforwardness, Noland's paintings are, finally, elusive. Their logic *seems* graspable, in part because of their clarity, in part because their structure *seems* rational, yet the paintings resist easy analysis because they are based entirely on intuitive, purely visual adjustments. Just as a Mondrian cannot be reduced to a set of mathematical, geometric ratios, a Noland cannot be described in terms of mere proportions or relations, nor even of color harmonies. Noland prizes this kind of elusiveness: ''You see things out of the corner of your mind or the corner of your eye that affect you just as strongly as things that you focus on, if not more so,'' he says.

II

From the late 1950s until relatively recently, Noland's painting could have been described, without too much oversimplification, as abstract Fauvism. While he clearly belongs to the entire history of Western art — his classicism embraces Poussin and David as well as their Greek and Roman prototypes — Noland, like many of the best American abstract painters of his generation, could be said to have taken Matisse's version of Fauvism as his point of departure. This is significant, since for many of the generation preceding Noland, Picasso remained of paramount importance, as he had been for the first American modernists of the twentieth century. This is not to say that Noland's work overtly resembles Matisse's (or any other Fauvist's), but the French master's radiant, thinly applied color, his lucid compositions, his distribution of attention across the surface of the canvas all inform Noland's work. Like Matisse and the Fauvists, Noland usually constructed his pictures out of discrete, brilliant, flat areas of color set side by side. Like the Fauvists, too, he consciously divorced himself from most of the concerns and techniques of traditional oil painting. He eschewed, as Matisse and his colleagues did, inflected paint handling and modulated color. The surface shifts of *alla prima* painting, like the tonal shifts of *chiaroscuro*, seemed linked to an old-fashioned tradition of illusionism. Paradoxically, they recalled, as well, orthodox Abstract Expressionism, as practiced by the generation preceding Noland, artists whose pictures depended on densely worked surfaces and dramatic contrasts of dark and light. Noland rejected equally the conventions of the remote past and of his own time in paintings notable both for their intense, close-valued colors and for their neutral, uninflected paint application.

Until about 1980, this description would have served for most of Noland's work. For all their declarative, legible structure, his pictures were as disembodied as "something that you heard." Their astonishing color appeared to have magically fallen into place; as though in order to appeal directly to the sense of sight, Noland had banished all sense of touch. Yet early in the 1980s, he began to explore media that depended utterly on touch: clay and handmade paper. Cast paper proved especially fascinating to him. Working with colored paper pulp forced him literally to move color around as a tactile substance, instead of applying it as a skin on a flat surface. (He once described the process as "making a picture out of colored cottage cheese.") It was a stimulating sensation. When he began to paint again soon after this experience, he found that he wanted the physicality of the cast paper works in his canvases. "I wanted to get expressive possibilities back into picture through the use of my hands or touch," Noland says.

In order to concentrate on what he called "a return to using the facility of the hand," Noland — typically — revived a format that he thoroughly understood, the "Chevron." He is not the first painter to mine his own past in this way. The American Cubist, Stuart Davis, for example, habitually reused images and structures that he found particularly fertile. For Davis, a telling "configuration," as he called it, could provide the armature for not one, but many works, made over a long period, with other images explored in between. Configurations from the 1920s form the basis of some of Davis's most ambitious pictures of the 1950s, firmly supported by the skeleton of a well understood composition, but newly conceived in terms of color and space.

For Noland, the "Chevron" format served a similar function. It was known but not exhausted; using it allowed him to think about other things. The "Chevrons" of the 1980s may hark back to structure conceived in the 1960s, but they read more as declarations of new obsessions than as continuations of earlier themes. The layout is familiar but everything else seems unprecedented. Surfaces are newly opulent; there is a new emphasis on layering and transparency, a new mutability of color. Part of this is purely technical.

Noland was testing the limits of state-of-the-art acrylic paint, seeing what he could do with "interference" colors that change according to the angle from which they are viewed, metallic powders, perlescent additives and the like. He was experimenting, too, with transparent gels that allow fluid, thin acrylic to be as responsive to the hand as thick oil paint. Yet this passion for materials was nothing new. Noland has always celebrated the characteristics of his media. He has never regarded paint as something to be overcome, but rather, as something to be exploited and celebrated to the fullest. He believes this is characteristic of the artists he admires the most: "Picasso," he says, "loved depicting. He didn't love painting. It's always more like filling in for Picasso. But you can see that Matisse *loved* the *stuff*. He loved making it thin, loved moving it around." As painting became more abstract, Noland believes, this kind of enthusiasm for materials became increasingly critical. "Abstract Expressionism — especially Pollock, not the more academic painters like de Kooning — made the threshold between illusion and the *stuff* of painting lower, the distance between them closer," Noland says. "Pollock made all things about the picture, all the *stuff*, actual. Taking the canvas off the stretcher, putting it on the floor, made it more real. Mixing up different kinds of paint, getting it to stain in, was getting at a kind of materiality."

That "materiality," Noland believes, was essential to the development of a new abstraction. "The allusions began to be more towards what the painting was made of, how it was made rather than towards subject matter. That became interesting enough that it was possible to eliminate having to make reference to all other subject matter considerations, all allusions beyond the physical reality of the picture. Morris Louis and I were interested in how Pollock and Helen Frankenthaler were using paint. Of necessity we had to get more interested in the stuff of painting. We talked a lot about whether to size the canvas or not to size, how to mix up paint."

These were not simply technical discussions, although the physical properties of various media certainly mattered. Magna, a kind of liquid lucite soluble in turpentine, one of the first plastic paints, was newly available in the 1950s and Noland and Louis found it worth investigating. "Magna had a different kind of quality from oil," Noland says, "You could thin it, stain with it. It would keep its intensity." The properties of Magna undoubtedly have something to do with the look of Louis's paintings of the 1950s and '60s, just as the properties of modern day acrylics have something to do with the characteristics of Noland's "Chevrons" of the 1980s, but material and physical qualities are only part of how we perceive these paintings. The 1980s "Chevrons" are radically new, unlike any of Noland's previous work — at least at first acquaintance — not only because of their seductively worked paint and nacreous colors, but because of their ambiguity. Despite their symmetry and geometry, the "rough Chevrons" appear to be momentary resolutions of infinite possibilities. Surfaces pulsate and shift; transparent layers of color remind us of previous states; paint application itself is varied and unpredictable. Even scale seems to be in flux, since intimate, eccentric marks within the color bands oppose the immediately graspable "Chevron" format to suggest new spatial complexities.

Yet for all their elusiveness, the most striking characteristic of the "rough Chevrons" may be their robust physicality, their sense of *madeness*. Unlike Noland's earlier works, which often appear to have come into being without conventional human intervention, through some extraordinary transsubstantiation of intuition and intelligence into image, the "rough Chevrons" bear dramatic evidence of Noland's touch. The paintings that established his reputation — the "Circles," the "Chevrons" and the "Stripes" — did not. They were restrained and evenhanded. Everything shared the same degree of saturation and smoothness, the same degree of dispassionateness. "Imagine," Noland says wryly, "keeping all that hidden for twenty years."

When Noland painted his first "Circles" in the late 1950s, they announced the beginning of a new "cool" approach (in Marshall MacLuhan's sense of the word) in American art, a new sense of detachment that proved to be an outstanding characteristic of much of what was subsequently produced in the 1960s and 1970s. The Pop artists of the 1960s and the minimalists who began to be conspicuous in the early '70s, for example, used imagery and themes wholly unlike Noland's but shared his fascination with "coolness," usually manifested in technical fastidiousness and a sense of distancing. All of this work, in particular, Noland's prophetic "Circles" of the late '50s, was startlingly different from the most acclaimed work that came before — Abstract Expressionism. Noland's "Circles"

Noland at work on "Rains" monotypes at the Mixografia Workshop, Los Angeles, 1985.

were especially different from the gestural, de Kooning-derived abstraction that was equated with serious art making at the time. The "Circles" were symmetrical, thinly painted, clear and bright at a time when advanced painting was supposed to be irregular, worked and full of dark and light contrasts. That their concentric bands of color were often brushy and varied in density seemed less important at the time (and for years afterward) than their clarity and limpidity. Noland himself helped us to ignore the evidence of his hand in his early work by emphasizing the immaculate aspects of the "Circles" in the paintings that followed them. We came to associate him almost exclusively with smoothly applied, disembodied color and exquisite, clean-edged surfaces.

The "rough Chevrons" of the 1980s make us read Noland's work somewhat differently. The "Circles," for example, now seem to prefigure the painterliness of Noland's recent work as much as they do the meticulousness of the "Chevrons" and "Stripes" that immediately followed them. It is easier to see now, too, that even the most rarefied of the "Stripes" are dependent upon nuances of surface: the subtle difference between bands of paint and the raw canvas against which they sit, or the surprise of two painted bands that touch in a picture where every other band is isolated by a strip of unpainted canvas. Similarly, it is now possible to see how the "Plaids" and the shaped canvases also anticipate some of Noland's more recent concerns. The contrast between dense bars of pigment and washy grounds, in these pictures, seems more significant in light of Noland's work of the past few years than it did when the series was first shown. In one group of "Plaids," the stained expanses of color are so lively that the overlying grid of color bars functions

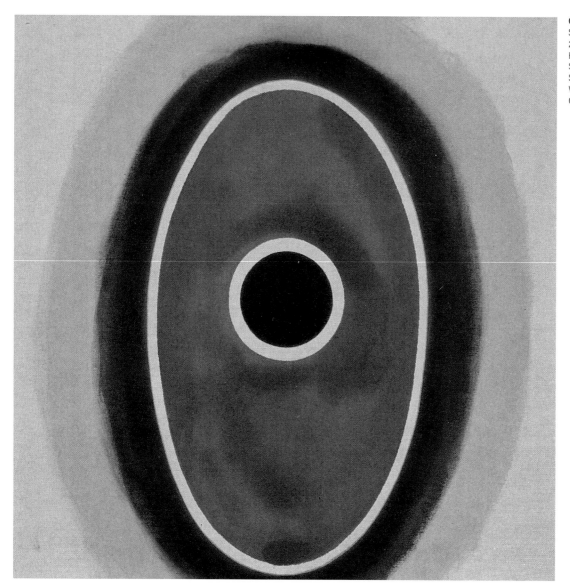

Columbus Egg. 1962.
Synthetic polymer,
22 × 22 in. (56 × 56 cm).
Hirshhorn Museum and
Sculpture Garden,
Smithsonian Istitution,
Washington D.C.
Gift of Josep H. Hishhorn.

like a kind of grille to keep the ground in check. Physical, as well as visual, unlikeness is emphasized. In a metaphysical sense, Noland has always exploited the variations in the visual weight of his colors, so it is hardly surprising to find him acutely sensitive to actual textures, no matter how subtle. The importance of delicate surface modulation in his earlier work is simply made easier to perceive by the sturdy physical presence of the "Chevrons" of the 1980s, but it has been there all along, a function of his dependence on the "stuff" of painting.

On the other hand, color in the "rough Chevrons" seems wholly new. Noland's palette, with its range of iridescent pinks and lilacs, icy blues and greens, florid reds and purples, is more overtly gorgeous than at any time in the past. Metallic blacks and dull golds, silvery greys and shimmering whites set off these lush hues, so that in contrast to the close-valued, relatively bright pictures of the 1960s and '70s, the "rough Chevrons" depend on dramatic shifts from bright to dark or neutral. Noland's seductive colors seem to have been dragged out of the surrounding darks and neutrals, wrestled to the surface by his insistent, repetitive touch. At the same time, these darks and neutrals, by penetrating the transparent colors of the bars, temper even his wildest chromatic flights. If it is true that in his earlier work Noland claimed color, with all its associative potency, for abstraction, then it is fair to say that in the "rough Chevrons" he did the same for *chiaroscuro*. In these pictures, the modulation of color from dark to light is detached from description and illusionism, just as surface inflection and touch itself are similarly set free. It is not an overstatement to say that the flourishes and flickering light of Baroque painting have been appropriated for abstraction in the "rough Chevrons."

Magic Box. 1959.
Acrylic on canvas,
96 × 96 in. (243.8 × 243.8 cm).
The Metropolitan Museum
of Arts, New York.
Anonymous gift.

In the end, however, even these most flamboyant of Noland's paintings share the "coolness" and detachment that have always characterized his work. The act of putting paint on a surface may be revealed in the "rough Chevrons" but it is abstracted, made, while not an end in itself, an autonomous element equal to any other element in the picture. Noland's handwriting, for all its insistent presence, is not a graph of emotion. Gesture and surface inflection serve primarily to modify color and to set up independent visual rhythms within the confines of particular zones of the "Chevron". They are not reflections of agitation. The "rough Chevrons" remain slightly reserved, distanced. Despite their ripe beauty, they are tougher than they seem at first acquaintance and more challenging.

At the same time that Noland was working on the "rough Chevrons," he was engaged in a project that demanded a very different way of thinking about painting, a commissioned mural for the Weisner Building at the Massachusetts Institute of Technology, by the architect, I.M. Pei. The mural occupied Noland from 1979 to 1985, a reasonable amount of time in an architect's schedule, but an eternity for a painter used to working as intuitively and directly as Noland. Perhaps the sensuality and the emphasis on *facture* in the "rough Chevrons" were partly a reaction against the necessary discipline of the M.I.T. project. In any event, the mural is as severely elegant as the "rough Chevrons" are lush.

Noland's mural wraps around the building, declaring itself modestly on the exterior with a few patches, then slides in, around corners, to expand to the full height of the walls of a glazed atrium before escaping out the other side. The mural's most brilliant hues are presented as a staccato arrangement of color blocks, inserted in the reveals between the aluminum panels that sheathe the building, to create a syncopated color web that is inextricably fused with the metal skin. The work declares itself slowly. First, the smallest units of color become visible: tightly contained squares and rectangles in bright, saturated hues. Next, the slightly larger, slightly less brilliant color bars come into play. Finally, the subtle color differences between the large aluminum panels themselves become apparent and the energetic but restrained pulse of the mural begins to alter our perceptions of the space. Noland's contribution is not simply decorative. The building is inconceivable without the mural's unpredictable flashes of color; the mural could not exist in any other context. It may be the most successful fusion of art and architecture since the 17th century.

"The possibility of dispersing colors through a given layout naturally appealed to me," Noland says. "The idea of putting a lot of color on the panel surfaces didn't. It would probably have been too strong an effect to live with. I wanted something more woven in. The interstices — that was suggested by I.M. Pei — suited me better because if one chose to look at them the eye would be moved along by the differences in color."

Oddly, Noland anticipated, to some extent, the character of the M.I.T. mural in his "Plaid" pictures of the 1970s. In these, he accented the places where vertical and horizontal bands cross to create a discontinuous rhythm very like that of the Weisner Building. This correspondence is not all that surprising, given Noland's habit of working out many different possibilities while apparently following one clearly defined path. What he calls "oddball" images persist throughout his career. Frequently the connection between them and the main body of his work seems obscure, but occasionally, an idea that didn't, in his words, appear to "go anywhere" will surface in unexpected ways, as important notions are bound to do. A recent flirtation with video art, the result of an invitation to work in the video department of the Pratt Institute, is characteristic. Noland began with a series of filmed images of a pond near his studio, later altered and enhanced by computer generated changes to forms and colors. The result bore little resemblance to landscape or nature, but surprisingly, recapitulated the scattered color patches of paintings Noland had made in the 1950s and abandoned. He had found them wanting in some way, never explored the series further and had, apparently, paid little attention to them since. Conceivably, something about the properties of video prompted him to recall images that he had rejected but had never entirely forgotten. The widely dispersed, varied pools of color in the undeveloped series of the 1950s may have seemed inappropriate to painting's stillness; the ability of video images to move may have provoked an unconscious recycling of the motif. Similarly, the accented intersections of the "Plaid" paintings' grids may have generated more energy than Noland felt their six foot squares or circles could comfortably contain. The M.I.T. mural allowed him to explore fully the implications of the syncopated geometry of the "Plaids" on a scale that he had never before attempted.

When it was first completed, in 1985, the M.I.T. mural, good as it was, seemed a self-sufficient "closed" project unrelated to what Noland was doing in his studio. He had responded to a particular set of circumstances with a particular solution derived from his past experience but not necessarily related to what currently preoccupied him. From about 1980 on, most of Noland's attention, no matter what his medium, was engaged not by discrete color relationships like those of the M.I.T. mural, but by the tension between neutral structure and exuberant surface. In his canvases, his cast paper pieces and especially in a series of large monotypes, aggressive textures, barely controlled by lucid geometric layouts, dominate almost to the point of supplanting chromatic color. In some of the monotypes, fragments of closely related hues intermingle to the point of reading as an especially subtle grey. If there is any link with the M.I.T. mural in these works, it is their physicality. The mural is painted, but in it Noland had to think of color as something tangibly inserted into an articulated structure, something that could be moved around in discrete, variable units, rather than something spread, like an intangible skin, across a flat surface. Differences between the mural and Noland's other work seem more significant than similarities, however. Just as the opulence of the "rough Chevrons" may have offered Noland an antidote to the rigors of producing the mural, the restrained color in the cast paper works and monotypes may simply have been a reaction to the demanding chromatic complexities of the mural. Whatever the motivation, it seemed clear that by the mid-80s, Noland's attention was firmly fixed on the new possibilities of color, surface and touch that he had begun to explore in the "rough Chevrons." The master of geometric clarity was engaged in becoming a master of the painterly.

III

The "rough Chevrons" were often outstanding pictures, but because Noland had chosen to reuse a structure that he had invented almost two decades earlier, they provoked questions. This is not to say that the format appeared exhausted or that using it signified a lack of inventiveness on Noland's part. Obviously, he was fully aware of the risks inherent in returning to a known composition; the decision had been deliberate and to judge by the evidence of the pictures, it had proved provocative and liberating. Nevertheless, even some of Noland's most ardent admirers sometimes wondered how long he could keep fresh a layout that he had already explored so thoroughly.

As the series developed, it became clear that the chevron still offered room for unexpected invention. A group of long horizontal pictures, for example, suggested that Noland was rethinking the possibilities of the configuration in fundamental ways. In some, he lined up several sets of nested V-shaped bars side by side, so that the small variations between apparently identical chevrons became overwhelmingly important; as in the horizontal "Stripes" of the late '60s, lateral extension — here reinforced and "measured" by repetition — was critical. In others of the series, Noland dissected the chevron itself, wrenching bars free of the V-shape, doubling and inverting them, stretching them to their limit. The result is an image related to the earlier "Chevrons" only in the most general way. Even when Noland adhered to a "traditional" centered version of the format, he often allowed linear drawing (as opposed to drawing implied by edges) to play a newly important role. The bones of the picture's construction were laid bare, exposed for the first time in Noland's work.

Those who worried that Noland might repeat himself need not have. The "Chevrons" of the 1980s separate themselves from their predecessors not only because of variations in composition and drawing, nor because of particularities of color and surface but because we perceive them differently. In the first "Chevrons" and their variants, the physical properties of paint and canvas seemed to be necessities rather than potentially expressive elements. Their painted bands existed as color first and as paint second. They were apparently integral with their support; when raw canvas showed between them, the smooth, thin paint of the bands seemed only fractionally more substantial than the woven fabric itself. There was little sense, in these pictures, that the chevron configuration was a figure on a background. Instead, the V-shaped bands and their support seemed perfectly congruent and coexistent. Like all of Noland's paintings until about 1980, the first "Chevrons" declared themselves as discrete but tangible objects that possessed the minimum physical means necessary to make them visible.

By contrast, the "rough Chevrons" of the 1980s are aggressively materialist. Their paint laden grounds are as substantial as their inflected bars. Instead of seeing the paintings as disembodied color *in* a surface, we perceive the "rough Chevrons" as a tactile colored substance *on* a support. Paradoxically, while these paintings read strongly as continuous, inflected surfaces, they also assert themselves as robust figures on almost equally robust grounds. In many of the series, color heightens this impression. In pictures with dark grounds, brighter, lighter bars detach themselves slightly from the sea of worked paint that surrounds them. In paintings with pale grounds, the relationship of bright and less bright is often reversed, but the sense of simultaneous continuity and separateness remains. Everything presses insistently forward.

The symmetrical, centered chevron format is critical to our perception of these pictures. A circle might have appeared too self-contained and have stamped itself out as

Kenneth Noland. Photo: Hans Namuth

a shape that subverted our sense of the canvas as a continuous whole; a chevron allowed to drift out of symmetry (as in earlier versions of the motif) might have weakened the sense of iconic confrontation. The spreading but contained symmetrical V, anchored at the corners of the canvas, simply reinforces the unignorable presentness of these pictures. Noland's insistence on *facture*, his revelation (at times) of construction drawing remind us, as well, of the history of each picture's making, rendering them generally more real and substantial. At the same time, each inflected bar declares itself as a unique *object*. Until the "rough Chevrons," Noland's paintings seemingly came into being without visible effort, all at once; the "rough Chevrons," quite the opposite, appear to have been constructed incrementally from a lexicon of discrete parts.

Noland's recent works make explicit these implications. They are constructed of large blocks of delicately modulated color, stacked vertically or horizontally. Strips of colored Plexiglass divide and punctuate the painted blocks, serving as color accents and, at the same time, creating subtle changes of level. Smaller, densely worked pictures explore related notions at a more intimate scale. In these, we are perhaps even more aware of their physical articulateness, since the Plexiglass strips are relatively large in relation to the painted planes and read not as linear drawing but as another kind of surface. The individual elements of the "rough Chevrons" only *seemed* distinct; Noland's new works are quite literally, made by assembling separate parts, each already distinguished by a particular shape, color, texture and density. Noland describes the process as "sculpting with color."

He explains: "They are made with hollow core doors as supports, which gives them human scale. They become slabs, chunks, pieces of color that I put together for pictorial works." It is as though the insubstantial color bands of his most famous pictures had detached themselves from their painted context and become physically distinct entities, sturdy pieces of color that Noland butts and piles. Once Noland has begun to assemble a group of blocks, their juxtaposition leads him to make alterations in color and (particularly in the most recent works in the series) radical adjustments in shape. Each element is influenced by or, in turn, influences its surroundings. The addition of a strip of color along an edge, for example, its length, its hue, its degree of projection, whether it is a Plexiglass strip or a painted one, all affect our perception of the total shape of the picture.

Though the recent pictures can best be characterized as constructions, they present themselves primarily as materially present paintings, not as flattened sculptures. They are, for all the complexity of their structure, principally about color, albeit color given virtually tangible form. While color is intimately bound up with the interrelationships of shape and surface, it dominates them, to some extent; in other words, color is never subjugated to structure nor used to emphasize structure. A phrase of David Smith's comes to mind. Noland's old friend spoke of combining painting and sculpture into a new art form that would "beat either one." Noland finds the relationship of hue and form to be a complex one: "Value differences in painting always cut in," he says. "Color differences always go side by side. Laterally. Color differences can illustrate three dimensional form, but using color in terms of hue belongs more properly to painting than modelling with dark and light does."

The stacked pictures range from exquisite orchestrations of lyrical pale hues to abrupt combinations of full-throttle near-primaries. Noland both exploits and undermines the particular qualities of his materials. In some pictures, he revels in the glossy surfaces of acrylic paint and plexiglass, teetering quite deliberately on the edge of vulgarity; in others, he tests the limits of subtlety and elegance, adjusting the smallest nuance of texture and hue. Several of the stacked pictures appear to depend on relatively specific but extremely abstract allusions to older art (although these are by no means their only associations). For example, three panels of chalky blue, creamy white and warm yellow immediately recall Vermeer, while a particular combination of matte red, pink and white is just as evocative of Matisse.

At first sight, Noland's recent stacked pictures seem noticeably unlike most of what preceded them, just as the "rough Chevrons" did, when they first appeared. Longer acquaintance, however, reveals the new paintings to be logical and probably inevitable descendants of Noland's earlier work. Their rich variety of surfaces is simply an intensification of the worked surfaces of the "rough Chevrons," made more tangible and literal by being stated in terms of the contrast between trowelled, loaded expanses and

Vermont. 1971-1973.
Wood, bronze
and corten steel,
145 × 135 × 167⅞ in.
(368.5 × 343 × 425 cm).
Tel Aviv Museum,
Tel Aviv, Israel.

thinly stained ones, between changes of level and changes of material, between translucency and opacity.

Shaping itself is hardly new for Noland. Noland feels that he has been aware of its possibilities almost from the beginning. ''Making the 'Circles','' he says, ''really had to do with shaping. I used a square very consciously. Shaping pictures in the 1950s was a slightly unconscious thing.'' Cropping — shaping the picture or, at least, deciding its limits as a separate step instead of working on a preexisting shape — has long been part of Noland's practice. He believes that cropping and shaping are integral to abstractness. They presuppose that the artist thinks of his picture as an independent object whose limits are determined only by aesthetic considerations, not by accepting a given set of proportions and dimensions.

''In the 1950s,'' Noland says, ''there was a kind of agreement that a good artist would do something in his picture that acknowledge the edge, but it was a question of doing something *when* you got to the edge. Cropping was something new. It came from photography and from Clement Greenberg. It was resisted as being too easy.''

The paintings of the mid-70s — the altered rectangles, the irregular hexagons and the slim ''Surfboards'' — overtly proposed alternatives to traditional painting shapes. Noland now says that he thought of the ''Surfboards'' as being ''almost like cut-out figures without being figurative.'' Their narrow length contains a memory of human proportion that anticipates the way the doors that make up his stacked pictures allude to the body. ''I think of them, in some way, as being like figures," Noland says, "They remind me of figures in vertical Cubist paintings. Even the small pictures have that kind of human proportion in the rectangles. It's not exactly a reference, but the relation of length to width in the rectangles is like a person."

It is conceivable that this abstracted allusion to the body derives, in part, from Noland's extended work on the M.I.T. mural — the project that had seemed unrelated to his evolving concerns with surface and texture at the time of its completion. His need to respond, in the mural, to the human scale given by the building's doors, windows and floor heights may have reawakened notions first explored in the "Surfboards." The "built" quality of the stacked pictures surely owes something to Noland's experience of architectural collaboration and it is what seems newest about the recent work. For apparently the first time, Noland no longer relies on a preestablished format as a point of departure, but allows the making of the picture to determine entirely its eventual size, shape and configuration. Only the fact of stacking or placing increments against one another remains constant; everything else is variable. Noland is well aware that he is working in a way unusual to him, but points out that his first shaped canvases were arrived at quite empirically, as were, to some extent, the "Plaids." "Before the 'Plaids,'" he says, "layouts got neutralized by repetition. There were more variables in the 'Plaids.' Each bar that went down determined what else I did."

For all their differences, what makes the stacked pictures immediately recognizable as intimately related to the "Circles" or the first "Chevrons" or the "Stripes" — in short, immediately recognizable as Nolands — is their inherent classicism, their transparency of composition. Since the 1950s, throughout all the variations in their layout, color and surfaces, Noland's paintings have borne witness to the presence of an ideal archetypical geometry, a Platonic absolute against which all variations are tested. Earlier in his career, Noland's classicism declared itself in terms of a restraint and dispassionateness that eventually helped to define our view of what was characteristic of painting of the '60s and early '70s. More recently, a new, intensified materiality has typified Noland's work, once again both a hallmark and response to what some art historians refer to as "the spirit of the times," but the sense of an underlying rational order has persisted.

For all his increasing fascination with the material substance of his paintings, Noland stresses the importance of the intangible: "All art that is expressive has to be illusionistic. The raw material out of which art is built is not necessarily in itself potent; you must transform it. Contours, tactility, touch, color, intervals, that's all part of the concreteness of art. You have to make the concreteness expressive. That way you don't cater to taste. You resist sentimentality. Things in a picture can't remind you too much of anything else. You have to resist all that."

Noland's resistance over the past three decades or so has produced a body of supremely elegant, eloquent and visually ravishing work. His own description of his experience of the art he admires most can stand as a useful definition of the effect Noland's best work can have. "When you look at a great painting," Noland says, "it's like a conversation. It has questions for you. It raises questions in you."

He adds, "Being an artist is about discovering things after you've done them. Like Cézanne — after twenty years of that mountain he found out what he was doing. If it isn't a process of discovery, it shows. I'm in it for the long haul."

CHRONOLOGY

Born 1924, Asheville, North Carolina.

Studied at Black Mountain College, North Carolina 1946-48, and with Ossip Zadkine in Paris 1948-49.

Taught at the Institute of Contemporary Art, Washington, D.C. 1949-51, at the Catholic University, Washington, D.C. 1951-60, and at the Washington Workshop Center of the Arts, 1952-56.

Elected to the American Academy and Institute of Arts and Letters, 1977.

On the Board of Trustees, Bennington College, Bennington, Vermont from 1985 to the present.

First Artist in Residence in Computer Video Arts, Pratt Institute, New York, September 1986 to April 1987.

Milton Avery Professor of the Arts, Bard College, Annandale-on-Hudson, New York, 1985.

Collaborated with I.M. Pei and Partners, Architects, on the Wiesner Building, Massachusets Institute of Technology, completed in 1985.

ONE MAN EXHIBITIONS

1949 Galerie Creuze, Paris.

1950 Watkins Gallery, American University, Washington, D.C.

1951 Dubin Gallery, Philadelphia.

1953 Dubin Gallery, Philadelphia.

1957 Tibor de Nagy Gallery, New York.

1958 Tibor de Nagy Gallery, New York.
Jefferson Place Gallery, Washington, D.C.

1959 French & Co., New York.

1960 Galleria dell'Ariete, Milan.
Jefferson Place Gallery, Washington, D.C.

1961 Andre Emmerich Gallery, New York.
The New Gallery, Bennington College, Bennington, Vermont
Galerie Neufville, Paris.

1962 Andre Emmerich Gallery, New York.
Galerie Charles Lienhard, Zurich.
Galerie Alfred Schmela, Dusseldorf.

1963 Kasmin Ltd., London.
Andre Emmerich Gallery, New York.
Galerie Lawrence, Paris.

1964 Andre Emmerich Gallery, New York.
Galerie Alfred Schmela, Dusseldorf.

1965 Jewish Museum, New York.
David Mirvish Gallery, Toronto.
Kasmin Ltd., London.

1966 Andre Emmerich Gallery, New York.
Nicholas Wilder Gallery, Los Angeles.

1967 Andre Emmerich Gallery, New York.

1968 Kasmin Ltd., London.
David Mirvish Gallery, Toronto.

1969 Lawrence Rubin Gallery, New York.

1971 Andre Emmerich Gallery, New York.

1972 Galerie Mikro.

1973 Andre Emmerich Gallery, New York.
Galerie Andre Emmerich, Zurich.
Waddinton Galleries, London.

1974 David Mirvish Gallery, Toronto.
Jack Glenn Gallery, Corona del Mar.
Janie C. Lee Gallery, Houston.
Rutland Gallery, London.

1975 Andre Emmerich Gallery, New York.
School of Visual Arts Gallery, New York.
Watson/deNagy & Co., Houston.

1976 Galerie Andre Emmerich, Zurich.
Galerie Daniel Templon, Paris.
Galerie Wentzel, Hamburg.
Leo Castelli Gallery, New York.
David Mirvish Gallery, Toronto.

1977 Thomas Segal Gallery, Boston.
Andre Emmerich Gallery, New York.
"Kenneth Noland: A Retrospective," Solomon R. Guggenheim Museum, New York, April 15-June 19, 1977; Hirshhorn Museum and Sculpture Garden and the Corcoran Gallery of Art, Washington, D.C. (jointly), October 1-November 27; Toledo Museum of Art, Toledo, Ohio, January-February 26, 1978; Denver Art Museum March 23-May 7, 1978.

1978 Andre Emmerich Gallery, New York (handmade paper works).
Medici-Berenson Gallery, Bay Harbor Islands, Florida.
Meredith Long & Co., Houston (handmade paper works).
The Parke-McCullough House, Vermont (handmade paper works).
Middendorf/Lane Gallery, Washington, D.C.
Waddington Graphics, London (handmade paper works).
Waddington Gallery, Montreal; Toronto, (handmade paper works).

1979 Galerie Andre Emmerich, Zurich.
Waddington Graphics, London (handmade paper works).
Thomas Segal Gallery, Boston (handmade paper works).
Waddington Galleries, Toronto (handmade paper works).
Castelli Graphics, New York.
Waddington Galleries, Montreal (handmade paper works).
Katonah Gallery, Katonah, New York (ceramics and handmade paper works).
Waddington Galleries, London.

1980 Castelli Graphics (Castelli Uptown), New York (handmade paper works).
Andre Emmerich Gallery, New York (handmade paper works).
Andre Emmerich Gallery, New York.
Ulrich Museum of Art, Wichita State University, Wichita, Kansas.
Aldrich Museum, Ridgefield, Connecticut.
Galerie Wentzel, Hamburg (handmade paper works).
Asher/Faure Gallery, Los Angeles (handmade paper works).

1981 Linda Farris Gallery, Seattle, Washington (handmade paper works).
Theo Waddington Gallery, Montreal (handmade paper works).
Andre Emmerich Gallery, New York.
Clarke-Benton Gallery, Santa Fe, New Mexico (handmade paper works).
Waddington Galleries, London.
Heath Gallery, Atlanta, Georgia (handmade paper works).

1982 Thomas Segal Gallery, Boston (monotypes).
Andre Emmerich Gallery, New York (monotypes).
Gimpel-Hanover & Andre Emmerich Galleien, Zurich.
Galerie Wentzel, Cologne, Germany.
Douglas Drake Gallery, Kansas City, Missouri (ceramic relief and handmade paper works).
Visual Arts Museum, New York (handmade paper works).
Downstairs Gallery, Edmonton, Alberta, Canada (handmade paper works).
Sandra K. Bertsch Gallery, Oyster Bay, New York.
B.R. Kornblatt Gallery, Washington, D.C. (handmade paper works).

1983 Andre Emmerich Gallery, New York.
Hokin Gallery, Inc. Bay Harbor Islands, Florida.
Duke University Museum of Art, Durham, North Carolina (handmade paper works).
Museo de Arte Moderno, Mexico, D.F.
Galerie Joan Prats, Barcelona (monotypes).

1984 Mixografia Gallery, Los Angeles.
Waddington & Shiell Galleries, Ltd., Toronto.
Galerie Joan Prats, New York (monotypes).
Galerie de France, Paris.
Galerie Villa Zanders, Bergisch Galdbach, West Germany.
Gallery 10, Inc. Scottsdale, Arizona (tapestries).
University Art Museum, University of California, Berkeley.
Galerie Reinhard Onnasch, Berlin, September 22-November 3.
Galerie Wentzel, Cologne, November-December.

Makler Gallery, Philadelphia, Pennsylvania, October 1-31 (monotypes).
Andre Emmerich Gallery, New York, December 6-29.

1985 Andre Emmerich Gallery, New York, March 6-30 (monotypes).
Galeria Joan Prats, Barcelona, May.
Gallery 10, New York, November 7 through January 4, 1986 (tapestries).
Andre Emmerich Gallery, New York, October 31-November 30.
Museo de Bellas Artes, Bilbao, Spain, September.
Diputacio de Valencia, Valencia, Spain, December.
Andre Emmerich Gallery, New York, April 3-26.

1986 Andre Emmerich Gallery, New York, April 3-26 (paintings).
R.H. Love Modern, Chicago, May 3-June 21.
Gallery One, Toronto, May 17-June 4 (handmade paper works).
Galeria Joan Prats, New York, June 5 (handmade paper works).
Robert Martin Gallery, Westchester Financial Center, White Plains, New York, June 19-July 10.

The Butler Institute of American Art, July 20-August 31, 1986.
Hunter Museum of Art, Chattanooga, Tennessee, November 9-January 4, 1986.
Satani Gallery, Tokyo, November 25-December 20.

1987 Galeria Joan Prats, New York, May 5.
Artist in Residence, Pratt Institute, New York, September 1986-1987.
Galerie Don Stewart, Montreal, October 2-20.

1988 Gallery One, Toronto, December 10-January 4, 1989.

1989 Hokin Gallery, Bay Harbor Islands, Florida, January 1989.
Salander-O'Reilly Galleries, Inc., New York, *Kenneth Noland: Paintings 1958-1989* September 5-October 27, 1989.

1990 Meredith Long & Co., Houston, January 9-February 2, 1990.
Helander Gallery, Palm Beach, Florida, February 7-March 3, 1990.

SELECTED BIBLIOGRAPHY

1965 Fried, Michael. Introduction to the catalogue, *Three American Painters*, Fogg Art Museum, Harvard University, Cambridge, 1965.

1967 Cone, Jane Harrison. "Kenneth Noland's New Paintings," *Artforum*, Vol. VI, November 1967.

Hudson, Andrew. "The 1967 Pittsburgh International," *Art International*, Vol. XI, Christmas 1967, pp. 57-64.

Kosloff, Max. *The Nation*, December 18, 1967, pp. 667-669.

Kramer, Hilton. Review, *The New York Times*, November 18, 1967.

1968 Ashton, Dore. "New York," review of AEG exhibition, *Studio International*, Vol. 175, February 1968, p. 93.

"Documenta IV, 1968," Kassel, Germany, 1968.

Greenberg, Clement. "Poetry of Vision," *Artforum*, Vol. VI, April 1968, pp. 20-21.

Krauss, Rosalind E. "On Frontality," *Artforum*, Vol. VI, May 1968, pp. 40-46.

Tillim, Sidney. "Evaluations and Re-Evaluations, A Season's End Miscellany...," *Artforum*, Vol. VI, Summer 1968, pp. 20-23.

Tillim, Sidney. "Scale and the Future of Moderism," *Artforum*, Vol. VI, October 1968, pp. 14-18.

Whitford, Frank and Robert Kudielka. "Documenta 4" A Critical Review, *Studio International*, Vol. 176, September 1968, pp. 74-78.

1969 Alley, Ronald. *Recent American Art*, Tate Gallery published by Order of the Trustees, 1969.

Ashton, Dore. *A Reading of Modern Art*, Cleveland and London, 1969, Part V, pp. 141-200.

Fried, Michael. "Recent Work by Kenneth Noland," *Artforum*, Vol. VII, Summer 1969, pp. 36-7.

1970 Bannard, Walter. "Notes on American Painting of the Sixties," *Artforum*, January 1970, pp. 40-45.

David Mirvish Gallery. *The Opening*, catalogue, September 1970.

Gouk, Alan. "An Essay on Painting," *Studio International*, Vol. 180, October 1970, p. 146.

Hudson, Andrew. *Ten Washington Artists: 1950-1970*, Edmonton Art Gallery, Edmonton, Canada, February 5-March 8, 1970, pp. 6-7, 10-11, 16-17.

1971 Bannard, Walter. "Noland's New Paintings," *Artforum*, Vol. X, November 1971, pp. 50-53.

Moffett, Kenworth. "Noland Vertical," *Art News*, Vol. 70, October 1971, p. 48.

Ratcliff, Carter. "New York Letter," *Art International*, Vol. XV, December 20, 1971, p. 59.

1972 Elderfield, John. "Abstract Painting in the Seventies," *Art International*, Vol. XVI, Summer 1972, p. 92.

1973 Moffett, Kenworth. "Noland," *Art International*, the Lugano Review, Vol. XVII, Summer 1973, pp. 22-33.

1974 Carmean, E.A., Jr. "The Great Decade American Abstraction/Modernist Art 1960-1970," exhibition catalogue, Museum of Fine Art, Houston, January 15-March 10, 1974. Color reproductions p. 12, plate 2, and p. 28, plate 8.

Carpenter, Ken. "To Re-Examine the Work of Kenneth Noland," *Studio International*, Vol. 187, July/August 1974.

1975 *Kenneth Noland*, exhibition catalogue, Edmonton, Alberta: Edmonton Art Gallery, March-April 1975, with essay by Karen Wilkin.

Russell, John. "Art: In Show of New Noland Paintings, Consistency Takes Unexpected Forms," The New York *Times*, November 22, 1975.

1976 Moffett, Kenworth. "Kenneth Noland's New Paintings and the Issue of Shaped Canvas," *Art International*, Vol. XX, April-May 1976.

1977 Diane Waldman. Color, Format and Abstract Art: An Interview with Kenneth Noland. *Art in America*, Vol. 65, May/June 1977, pp. 99-105.

Glueck, Grace. The 20th Century Artists Most Admired by Other Artists, *Art News*, Vol. 77, November 1977, p. 78.

Hess, Thomas B. "Kenneth Noland, Hesitant Prophet," *New York Magazine*, May 23, 1977, pp. 76-78.

Hilton Kramer. "Art: Landmarks On the Color Field," *New York Times*, April 22, 1977.

Hudson, Andrew. "Washington: Matisse's Influence," *Artmagazine* (Toronto), Vol. 9, December/January/February 1977-78, pp. 12-17.

Kenneth Noland: A Retrospective, Solomon R. Guggenheim Museum, New York, 1977, text by Diane Waldman.

Moffett, Kenworth. *Kenneth Noland*, New York: Harry N. Abrams, Publishers, Inc. 1977, 240 pages, 233 plates.

Polcari, Stephen. "Kenneth Noland: Independence in the Face of Conformity," *Art News*, Vol. 76, Summer 1977, pp. 153-155.

Robert Hughes. "Pure Uncluttered Hedonism," *Time Magazine*, May 2, 1977.

1978 Goldman, Judith. *Kenneth Noland Handmade Papers*, Tyler Graphics Ltd., Bedford Village, New York, 1978.

Hudson, Andrew. *Fifteen Sculptors in Steel Around Bennington, 1963-1978*, Park-McCullough House Association, North Bennington, Vermont, 1978.

Lussier, Real. *Artistes Americains Contemporains*, catalogue for the exhibition organized by the Musee d'Art Contemporain, Montreal, 1978.

1979 Cavaliere, Barbara. "Kenneth Noland," *Arts Magazine*, Vol. 53, January 1979, p. 20.

Color Abstractions: Selections from the Museum of Fine Arts, Boston, exhibition catalogue, Federal Reserve Bank of Boston Display Area, 1979, introduction by Kenworth Moffett.

Gerritt, Henry. "Paper in Transition," *The Print Collector's Newsletter*, Vol. X, July-August 1979, p. 84.

Louisiana: Pictorial Reportage, catalogue of the Louisiana Museum of Modern Art, Humlebaek, Denmark, 1979, pp. 62, 89.

Mackie, Alwynne. "Kenneth Noland and Quality in Art," *Art International*, Vol. 23, Summer 1979, pp. 40-45, 52-53.

Malerei des zwanzigsten Jahrhunderts, Kunstsammlung Nordrhein-Westfalen, Dusseldorf, 1979; Noland, pp. 43-44.

Schwartz, Ellen, Review, "Kenneth Noland," Andre Emmerich Gallery, *Art News*, Vol. 78, January 1979, p. 138.

1980   *L'Amerique aux Independants*, Société des Artistes, Grand Palais, Paris, 1980, pp. 37, 98.

1981   *Helen Frankenthaler Morris Louis/Kenneth Noland/Jules Olitski: Depuis la Couleur, 1958/1964*, Bordeaux: Centre d'Arts Plastiques Contemporains, 1981, essay by Dominique Fourcade.

Westkunst, exhibition catalogue, Museen der Stadt Köln, 1981, text by Laszlo Glozer; pp. 268-70, 459.

1982   *A Private Vision: Contemporary Art from the Graham Gund Collection*, Museum of Fine Arts, Boston, 1982; with essay by Kenworth Moffett on Ken Noland, p. 10, reproductions pp. 36-39.

American Artists on Art from 1940 to 1980, edited by Ellen H. Johnson, New York: Harper & Row, Publishers, 1982, pp. 47-50.

Ameringer, Will. "Kenneth Noland," *Arts*, Vol. 56, May 1982, p. 3.

1983   Moure, Gloria. "Kenneth Noland: Denoting Color," *Arte*, January 9, 1983. (English translation also.)

Kenneth Noland: Monotipos, Barcelona 1983, Barcelona: Ediciones Polígrafa, 1983.

Kenneth Noland: Recent Paperworks, exhibition catalogue, Duke University Museum of Art, Durham, North Carolina, 1983, with essay by Elizabeth Higdon.

Kenneth Noland "Vientos" (Winds), exhibition catalogue, Museo de Arte Moderno, Mexico City, Mexico, June-September, 1983. Mexico City: Taller de Gráfica Maxicana, Mexico City, with essay by Henry Geldzahler.

Kenneth Noland: Winds, Painted Monotypes, exhibition catalogue, Andre Emmerich Gallery, New York, November 10-December 3, 1983; with essay by Henry Geldzahler.

Russell, John. "Monotypes by Kenneth Noland," *The New York Times*, November 18, 1983, p. C26.

Talley, Charles. "The Navajo Tapestry: A Medium of Exchange," *Craft International*, April 1983, pp. 16-20.

The American Artists as Printmaker, exhibition catalogue, The Brooklyn Museum, 23rd National Print Exhibition, October 28, 1983-January 22, 1984, with essay by Barry Walker, p. 94.

1984   *Arte Contemporáneo Norteamericano, Colección David Mirvish*, exhibition catalogue, American Embassy in Madrid, January 1984, p. 40.

Kenneth Noland in Paris, 1984, exhibition catalogue, Galerie de France, June 1984, with essay by Ann Hindry.

"Kenneth Noland: Winds, Painted Monotypes," *The Print Collector's Newsletter*, January-February 1984, p. 217.

McCabe, Cynthia Jaffe. *Artistic Collaboration in the Twentieth Century*, exhibition catalogue, Hirshhorn Museum and Sculpture Garden, Washington D.C., 1984, pp. 169-170.

Peppiatt, Michael. "Sujet Tabou: Exposition Risquee," *Connaissance des Arts*, September 1984, No. 391, with color reproduction on p. 87.

Wilkin, Karen. "Kenneth Noland: Sensual Made Visible," *Art Press*, Issue No. 83, July-August 1984, pp. 24-26.

1985   "Artists and Architects Collaborate: Designing the Weisner Building," Boston: MIT Committee of Visual Arts, 1985. Interview with Kenneth Noland, pp. 69-78. Description of collaborative project by Jeffrey Cruikshank and Robert Campbell, pp. 15-16. Color reproduction of collaboration on front and back covers and black and white reproductions, pp. 16, 18, 68, 70.

Debrowski, Magdalena. "Contrasts of Form, Geometric Abstract Art," 1910-1980, exhibition catalogue, Museum of Modern Art, New York, 1985, with color reproduction, p. 233.

"New York New Art Now 85, ARCA Marseille," exhibition catalogue, ARCA Centre d'Art Contemporain, Marseille, July 9-August 31, 1985, with introduction by Roger Pailhas. Color reproduction, p. 81.

"Pre Postmodern, Good in the Art of Our Time," exhibition catalogue, Richard F. Brush Art Gallery, St. Lawrence University, 1985. Color reproduction, p. 11.

"Selections from the William J. Hokin Collection," exhibition catalogue, Museum of Contemporary Art, Chicago, 1985, plates 84-91.

"The Painter's Music, The Musician's Art," Program for premiere performance by An Die Musik in collaboration with Helen Frankenthaler, David Hockney, Robert Motherwell, and Kenneth Noland. Solomon R. Guggenheim Museum, New York, Sunday, November 17, 1985.

"The Wiesner Building," architectural catalogue, The Wiesner Building at The Massachusetts Institute of Technology, Cambridge, Massachusetts, 1985. Colour reproductions on pp. 2-4.

Tuchman, Phyllis. "Architectural Digest Visits Kenneth Noland," *Architectural Digest*, Vol. 42, July 1985, plates 110-115. Photographs by Hans Namuth.

Tuchman, Phyllis. "Kenneth Noland," *Architectural Digest*, Vol. 42, July 1985, pp. 110-115 & 149.

Upright, Diane. "Grand Compositions: Selections from the Collection of David Mirvish," exhibition catalogue, The Fort Worth Art Museum, Fort Worth, Texas, March 10-May 1, 1985, with seven color reproductions.

1986   *Kenneth Noland*, exhibition catalogue, Japan: Satani Gallery, Tokyo, November 25-January 20, 1986, with essay by Karen Wilkin.

"Kenneth Noland, Rains: Painted Monotypes," exhibition catalogue, Galery One, Toronto, 1986.

Moffett, Kenworth. "Kenneth Noland," *Moffett's Artletter*, May 1986, p. 1.

Tillim, Sidney. "Abstraction Revisited," *Art in America*, Vol. 74, April 1986, pp. 166-167.

1988   Wilkin, Karen. "Artist's Dialogue: Kenneth Noland," *Architectural Digest*, Vol. 45, March 1988.

MAJOR MUSEUM COLLECTIONS

Albright-Knox Gallery, Buffalo, New York
Art Institute of Chicago, Illinois
Baltimore Museum of Art, Maryland
City Art Museum, St. Louis, Missouri
Columbus Gallery of Fine Arts, Ohio
Corcoran Gallery of Art, Washington, D.C.
Des Moines Art Center, Iowa
Detroit Institute of Fine Arts, Michigan
Fogg Art Museum, Cambridge, Massachusetts
Solomon R. Guggenheim Museum, New York
Hirshhorn Museum and Sculpture Garden, Washington, D.C.
Honolulu Academy of Arts, Hawaii
Los Angeles County Museum of Art, California
Metropolitan Museum of Art, New York
Milwaukee Art Center, Wisconsin
Museum of Fine Arts, Boston, Massachusetts
Museum of Modern Art, New York

National Gallery of Art, Washington, D.C.
Pasadena Art Museum, California
Phillips Collection, Washington, D.C.
Rose Art Museum, Brandeis University, Waltham, Massachusetts
Walker Art Center, Minneapolis, Minnesota
Whitney Museum of American Art, New York

Australian National Gallery, Canberra
Gallery of South Australia, Adelaide
Hara Museum of Contemporary Art, Tokyo
Kunsthaus, Zurich
Kunstmuseum, Basel
Kunstsammlung Nordrhein-Westfalen, Dusseldorf
Louisiana Museum, Humlebaek, Denmark
Musee National d'Art Moderne, Centre National d'Art et de Culture
Georges Pompidou, Paris
Stedelijk Museum, Amsterdam
Tate Gallery, London

1. **Luster.** 1958.
   Magna on canvas, 59 × 59 in. (149.8 × 149.8 cm).
   Private collection.

2. **This.** 1958-1959.
Acrylic on canvas, 84 × 84 in. (213.3 × 213.3 cm).
Courtesy Salander-O'Reilly Galleries, New York.

3. **That.** 1958-1959.
   Acrylic on canvas, 81¾ × 81¾ in. (207.6 × 207.6 cm).
   Mr. and Mrs. David Mirvish Collection, Toronto.

4. **Untitled.** 1959.
Acrylic on canvas, 33¾ × 33¾ in. (85.7 × 85.7 cm).
Courtesy Salander-O'Reilly Galleries, New York.

5. **Fête.** 1959.
   Magna on canvas, 69 × 70 in. (175.2 × 177.8 cm).
   Courtesy Salander-O'Reilly Galleries, New York.

6

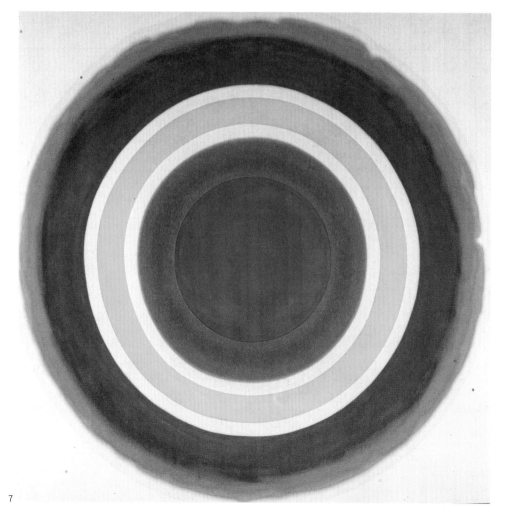

7

6. **Whirl.** 1960.
   Acrylic on canvas, 70¾ × 69½ in. (179.7 × 176.5 cm).
   Coffin Fine Arts Trust Fund, 1974; Nathan Emory Coffin Collection
   of the Des Moines Center, New York.

7. **Bloom.** 1960.
   Acrylic on canvas, 66⅜ × 67⅛ in. (170 × 171 cm).
   Kunstsammlung Nordrhein-Westfalen, Düsseldorf.

8. **Earthen Bound.** 1960.
   Acrylic on canvas, 103¼ × 103¼ in. (262.2 × 262.2 cm).
   Collection of the artist.
   Courtesy Salander-O'Reilly Galleries, New York.

9. **The Nightingale.** 1960.
   Acrylic on canvas, 68½ × 68½ in. (174 × 174 cm).
   Mr. and Mrs. Arthur Rock Collection.

10. **Nieuport.** 1960.
    Acrylic on canvas, 68½ × 68½ in. (174 × 174 cm).
    Art Gallery of Ontario, Toronto.
    Photo: Karol Ike

11. **Flutter.** 1960.
    Oil on canvas, 67 × 67¼ in. (170.2 × 170.8 cm).
    Steve Martin Collection.

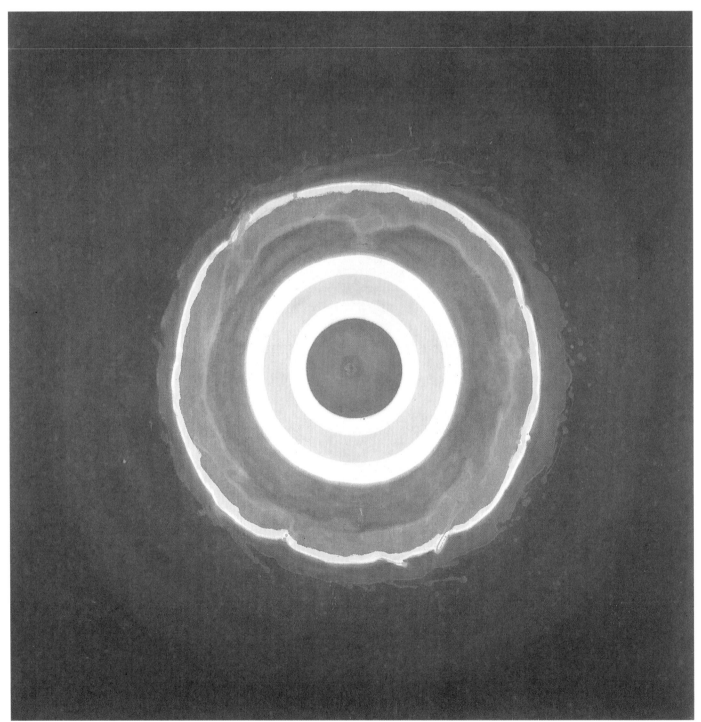

9

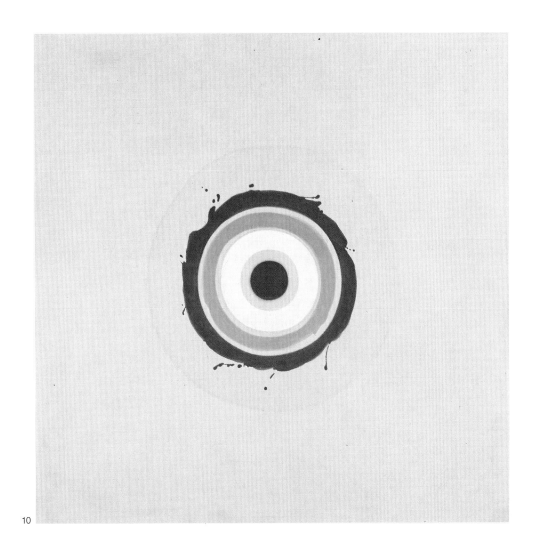

10

11

12. **Inner Way.** 1961.
Acrylic on canvas, 83 × 83 in. (210.8 × 210.8 cm).
Mr. and Mrs. Graham Gund Collection, Cambridge, Mass.

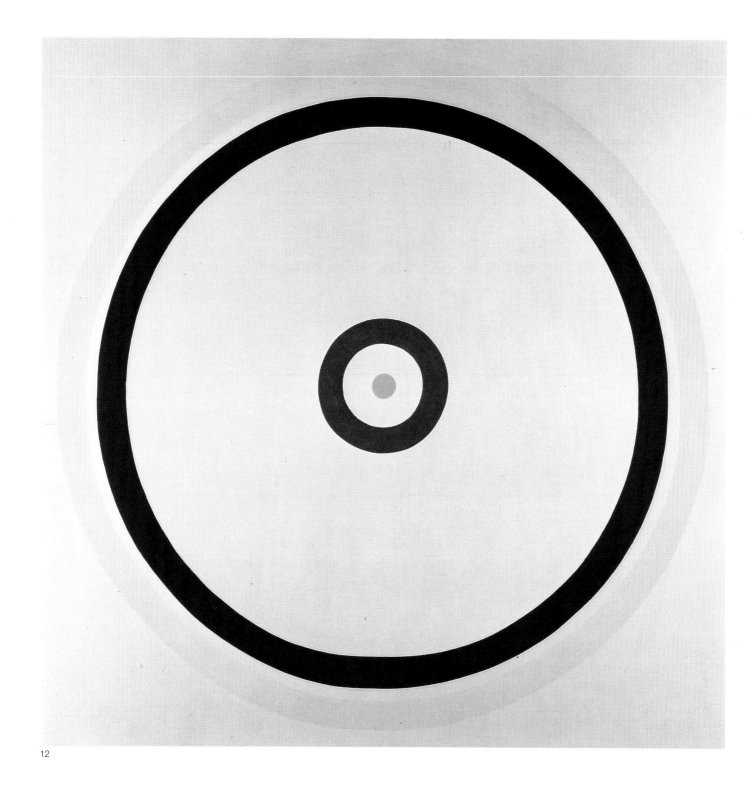

13. **Turnsole.** 1961.
Synthetic polymer paint on canvas, 94⅛ × 94¼ in. (239 × 239 cm).
Collection, The Museum of Modern Art, New York. Blanchette Rockefeller Fund.

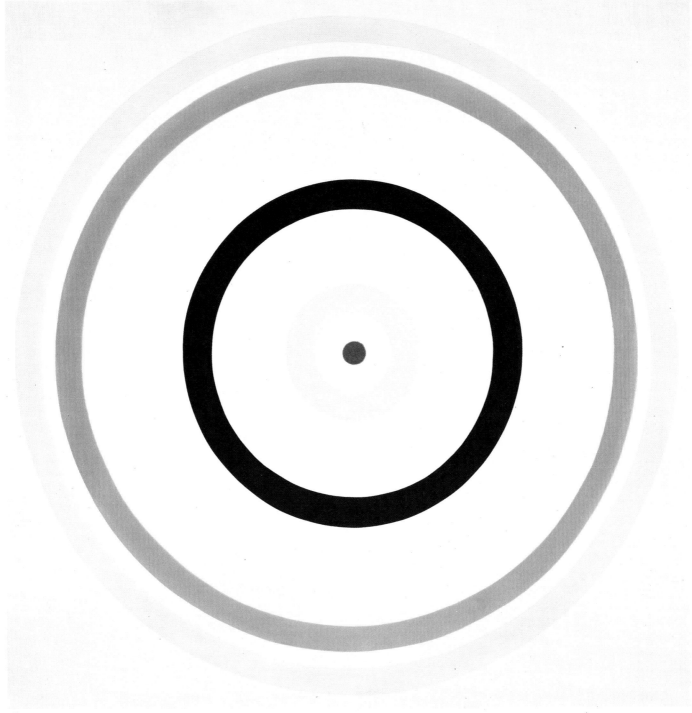

13

14. **Winter Sun.** 1962.
Acrylic on canvas with Plexiglass, 69¾ × 69½ in. (177 × 176.5 cm).
Emanuel Hoffman-Foundation, Museum für Gegenwartskunst Basilea.

15. **Matter of Midnight.** 1963.
   Acrylic on canvas, 72 × 72 in. (182.8 × 182.8 cm).
   Collection of the David Mirvish Gallery, Toronto.

16. **Dusk.** 1963.
   Synthetic polymer on canvas, 94¾ × 76 in. (240.8 × 193.1 cm).
   Hirshhorn Museum and Sculpture Garden Smithsonian Institution.
   Gift of Joseph H. Hirshhorn, 1966.

17. **Red, White and Green.** 1963.
    Acrylic on canvas, 80¾ × 117⅜ in. (205 × 298 cm).
    Courtesy Salander-O'Reilly Galleries, New York.

17

18. **Bend Sinister.** 1964.
    Synthetic polymer on canvas, 92½ × 162½ in. (235 × 411.5 cm).
    Hirshhorn Museum and Sculpture Garden Smithsonian Institution.
    Gift of Joseph H. Hirshhorn, 1966.

19. **And Again.** 1964.
Acrylic on canvas, 69 × 69 in. (175.2 × 175.2 cm).
Mr. and Mrs. Bagley Wright Collection.

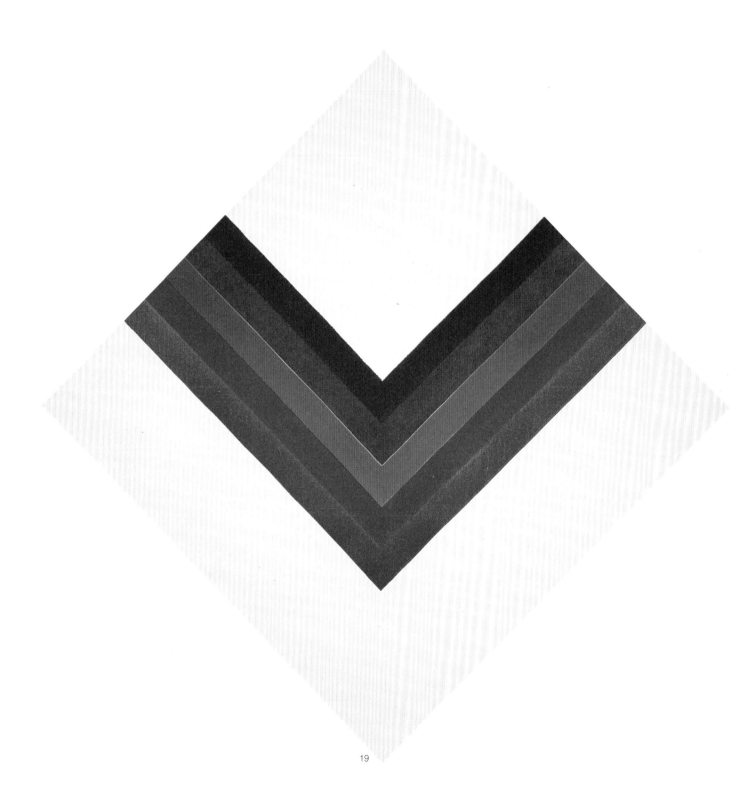

20. **C.** 1964.
Acrylic plastic on canvas, 69¾ × 69¾ in. (177.2 × 177.2 cm).
Art Gallery of Ontario, Toronto. Gift from Corporations Subscription Fund, 1965.
Photo: Carlo Catenazzi.

21. **Blue Plus Eight.** 1964.
Acrylic on canvas, 69½ × 69½ in. (176.5 × 176.5 cm).
Collection of the David Mirvish Gallery, Toronto.

22. **Plunge**. 1965.
    Acrylic on canvas, 48 × 48 in. (122 × 122 cm).
    Mrs. Anne Mirvish Collection, Toronto.

23. **No Bid.** 1965.
Acrylic on canvas, 46 × 46 in. (117 × 117 cm).
Private collection, Toronto.

23

24. **Dark Sweet Cherry.** 1966.
Acrylic on canvas, 60 × 86 in. (152.4 × 218.5 cm).
Collection of the David Mirvish Gallery, Toronto.

24

25. **Grave Light.** 1965.
   Acrylic on canvas, 102 × 210 in. (259 × 533 cm).
   The Gund Art Foundation.

26. **Untitled.** 1965.
Acrylic on canvas, 63½ × 63½ in. (161.2 × 161.2 cm).
Private collection.

26

27. **Greenbrier.** 1966.
     Acrylic on canvas, 24 × 69 in. (61 × 175.2 cm).
     Courtesy Salander-O'Reilly Galleries, New York.

28. **Untitled.** 1966.
Acrylic on canvas, 96 × 24 in. (243.8 × 61 cm).
Private collection.

28

29. **Must.** 1966.
Acrylic on canvas, 48 × 96 in. (121.9 × 243.8 cm).
Collection of The Edmonton Art Gallery, Alberta. Donated by Westburne Int. Ind.

29

30. **Jump.** 1966.
Acrylic on canvas, 35 × 120 in. (88.9 × 305 cm).
Collection of the David Mirvish Gallery, Toronto.

31. **Shade.** 1966.
Acrylic on canvas, 24 × 96 in. (61 × 243.8 cm).
Mr. and Mrs. David Mirvish Collection, Toronto.

30

31

32. **Approach.** 1966.
Acrylic on canvas, 96 × 22 in. (243.8 × 56 cm).
Private collection.

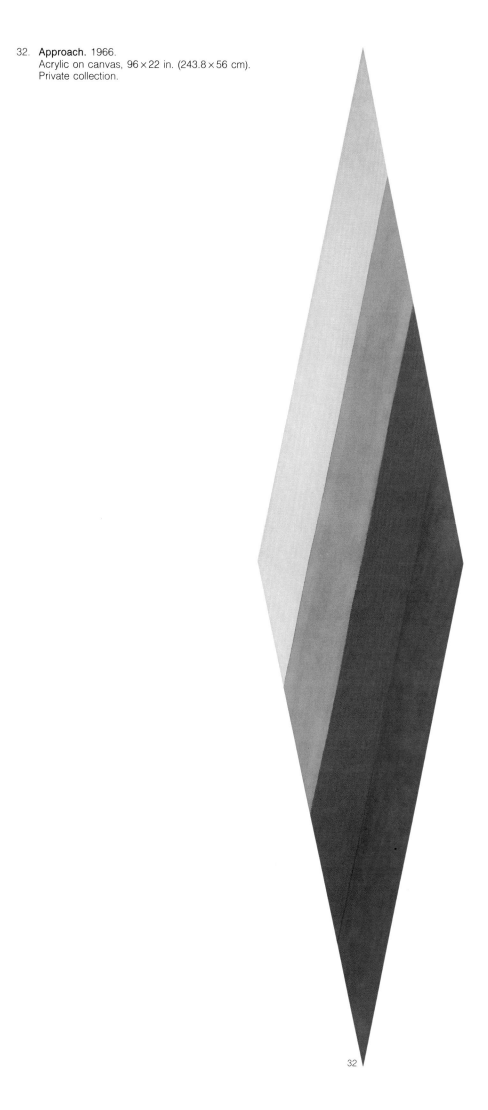

33. **Pause.** 1966.
Acrylic on canvas, 36 × 102 in. (91.4 × 259.1 cm).
Private collection.
Photo: Mick Hales.

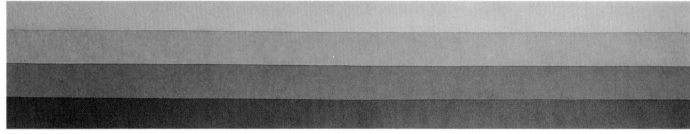

33

34. **In the Curl.** 1967.
   Acrylic on canvas, 96 × 24 in. (243.8 × 61 cm).
   Courtesy Salander-O'Reilly Galleries, New York.

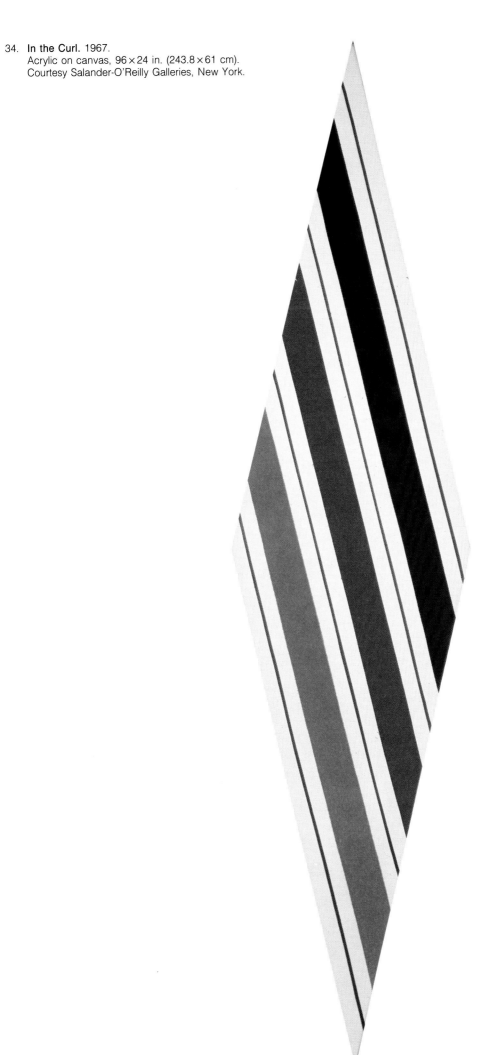

34

35. **Magus.** 1967.
   Acrylic on canvas, 86½ × 270 in. (219.7 × 685.5 cm).
   Collection of the David Mirvish Gallery, Toronto.

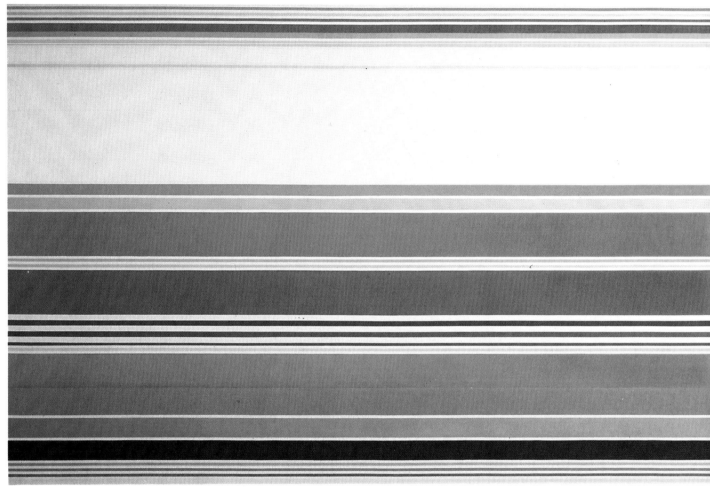

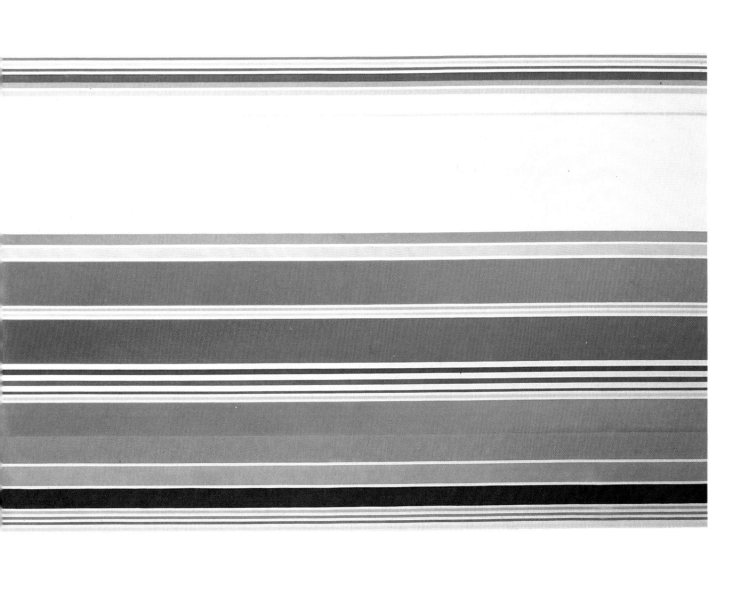

36. **Via Token.** 1969.
Acrylic on canvas, 100¼ × 240 in. (254.6 × 610 cm).
Collection of the David Mirvish Gallery, Toronto.

37. **Via Tradewind.** 1968.
Acrylic on canvas, 53 × 114 in. (134.6 × 289.5 cm).
Dr. and Mrs. Paul Tunick Collection, New York.
Photo: Silvia Sarner.

38. **Mexican Camino.** 1970.
Acrylic on canvas, 164 × 44 in. (416.5 × 111.7 cm).
Mr. and Mrs. Harry W. Anderson Collection, Atherton, Ca.

38

39. **Brief Rhythm.** 1971.
Acrylic on canvas, 58½ × 56⅛ in. (148.5 × 142.5 cm).
Courtesy Salander-O'Reilly Galleries, New York.

40. **Sutters Mill.** 1971.
Acrylic on canvas, 91¾ × 31½ in. (233 × 80 cm).
Mr. and Mrs. Michael Steiner Collection.

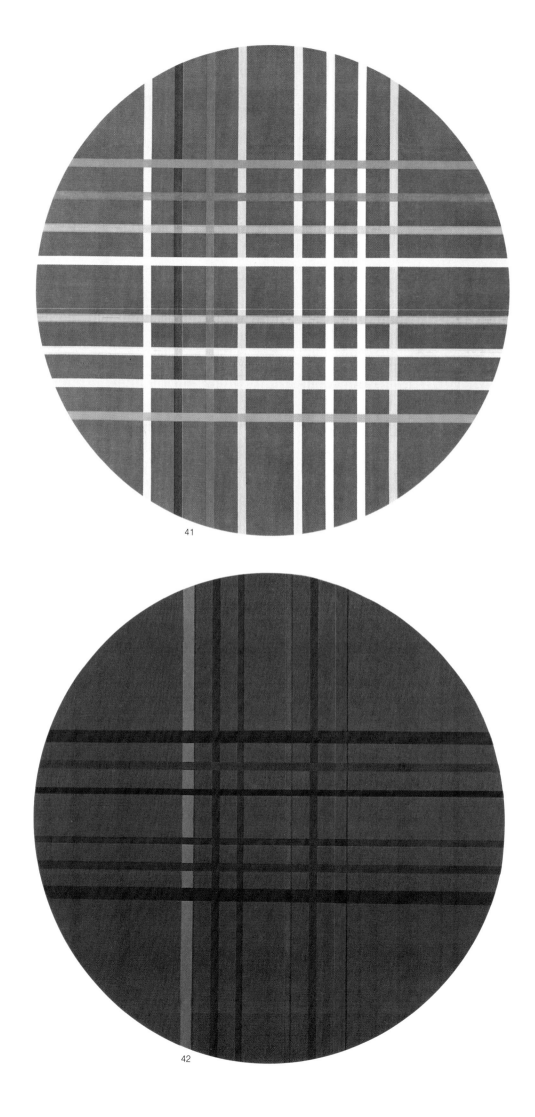

41

42

41. **Circum Grid Green.** 1973.
Acrylic on canvas, 79 in. (200.6 cm) diameter.
Collection of the David Mirvish Gallery, Toronto.

42. **Paralax.** 1973.
Acrylic on canvas, 79 in. (200.6 cm) diameter.
Collection of the David Mirvish Gallery, Toronto.

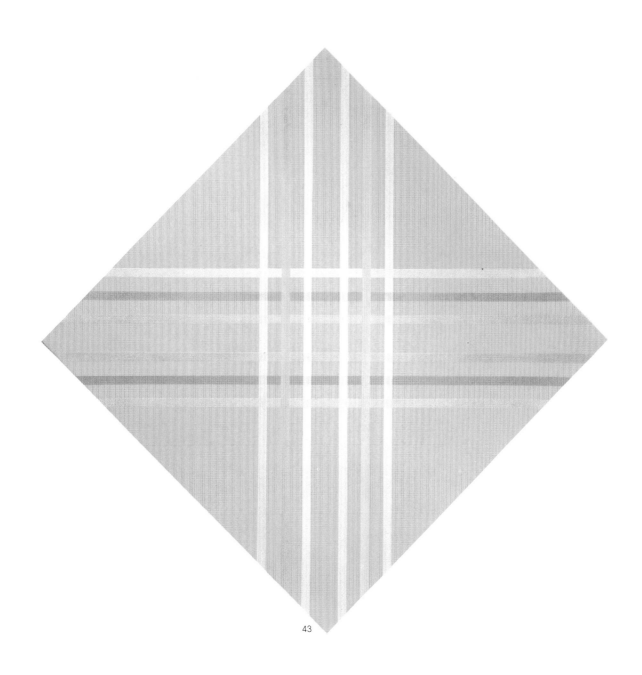

43

43. **Reigning Rule.** 1973.
Acrylic on canvas, 74¼ × 74¼ in. (188.5 × 188.5 cm).
Collection of the David Mirvish Gallery, Toronto.

44. **Burnt Beige.** 1975.
Acrylic on canvas, 112 × 95½ in. (284.5 × 242.5 cm).
Leo Castelli, New York.

44

45. **Ova Ray.** 1976.
   Acrylic on canvas, 85 × 106¾ in. (215.8 × 271 cm).
   Collection of the artist.
   Courtesy Salander-O'Reilly Galleries, New York.
   Photo: Steven Sloman.

45

46. **Moon Ray.** 1976.
    Acrylic on canvas, 63¼ × 84¾ in. (160.6 × 215.2 cm).
    Collection of the artist.
    Courtesy Salander-O'Reilly Galleries, New York.
    Photo: Steven Sloman.

46

47. **Field of Green.** 1977.
    Acrylic on canvas, 65½ × 98½ in. (166.3 × 250 cm).
    Courtesy Salander-O'Reilly Galleries, New York.

47

48. **C and H.** 1977.
   Acrylic on canvas, 60 × 90 in. (152.3 × 228.5 cm).
   Collection of the artist.
   Courtesy Salander-O'Reilly Galleries, New York.
   Photo: Steven Sloman.

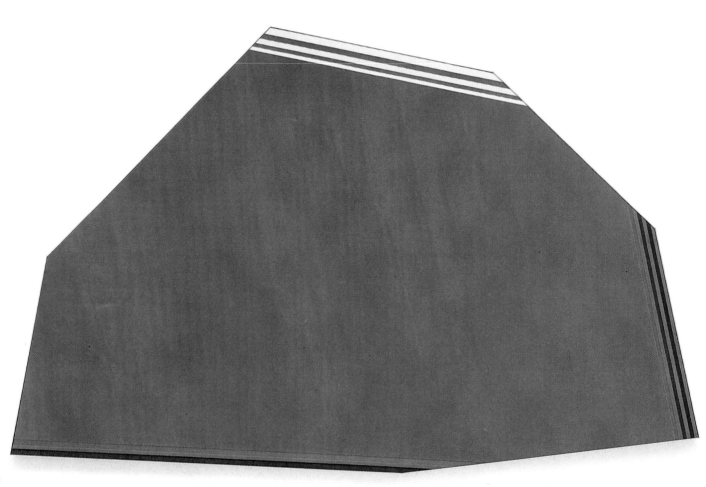

48

49. **Turns.** 1977.
Acrylic on canvas, 69¾ × 94¾ in. (177 × 240.6 cm).
Courtesy Salander-O'Reilly Galleries, New York.

49

50. **Rejoin.** 1980.
Acrylic on canvas, 74½ × 162½ in. (189 × 412.5 cm).
Collection of the artist.
Courtesy Salander-O'Reilly Galleries, New York.
Photo: Steven Sloman.

50

51. **Sweet Box**. 1978.
   Acrylic on canvas, 61 × 71 in. (155 × 180.3 cm).
   Private collection, Sioux City, Iowa.

51

52. **Adjoin.** 1980.
Acrylic on canvas, 88½ × 178¾ in. (224.7 × 454 cm), irregular.
Mr. and Mrs. Graham Gund Collection.
Photo: Greg Heins.

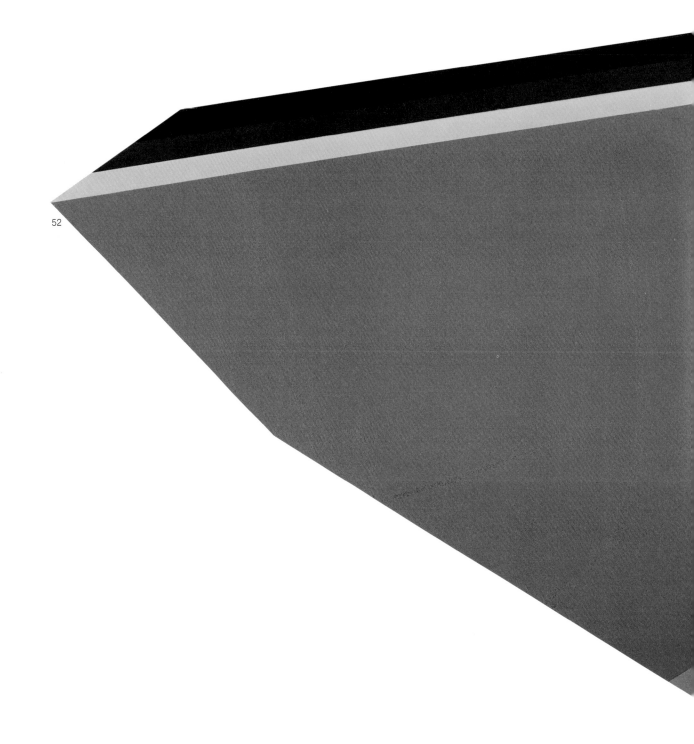

52

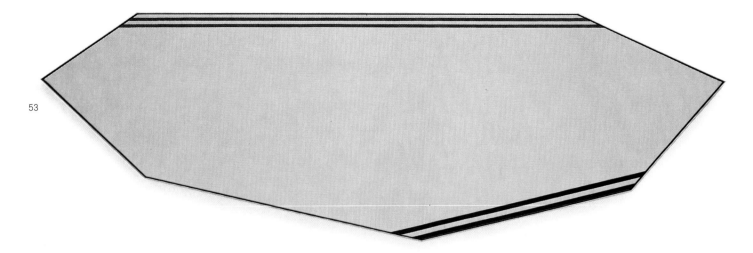

53

54

53. **Occurent.** 1979.
Acrylic on canvas, 36¾ × 114¼ in. (93.3 × 290.2 cm).
Collection of the artist.
Courtesy Salander-O'Reilly Galleries, New York.
Photo: Steven Sloman.

54. **Vessel.** 1980.
Acrylic on canvas, 79½ × 166 in. (202 × 421.6 cm).
Private collection.
Photo: Steve Sloman.

55

55. **Second.** 1979.
Acrylic on canvas, 39⅜ × 107¾ in. (100 × 273.7 cm).
A. J. Pyrch Collection, Victoria B.C.

56. **Silver.** 1980.
Acrylic on canvas, 95½ × 19⅛ in. (242.5 × 48.6 cm).
Roger Diener Collection, Basel.

57. **Flare.** 1981.
Acrylic on canvas, 22 × 92 in. (55.9 × 233.7 cm).
Dr. and Mrs. Everett Ref Collection.

56

57

58. **Apace.** 1981.
Acrylic on canvas, 79½ × 32½ in. (202 × 82.5 cm).
Lisa Dennison Collection.

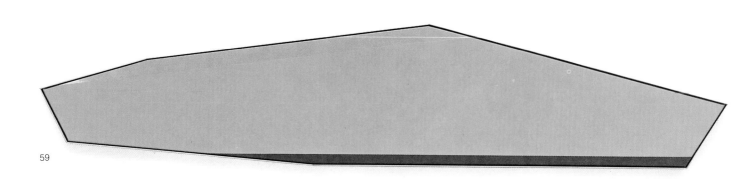

59

59. **Begin and End.** 1981.
Acrylic on canvas, 19³/₈ × 96¹/₂ in. (49 × 245 cm).
Collection of the artist.
Courtesy Salander-O'Reilly Galleries, New York.
Photo: Steven Sloman.

60

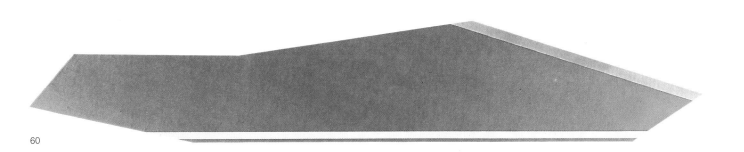

60. **Reppearance**. 1981.
   Acrylic on canvas, 17½ × 99 in. (44.5 × 251.5 cm).
   Courtesy Salander-O'Reilly Galleries, New York.

61

61. **Silver Shade.** 1982.
Acrylic on canvas, 17 × 81 in. (43.2 × 205.7 cm).
Collection of the artist.
Courtesy Salander-O'Reilly Galleries, New York.
Photo: Steven Sloman.

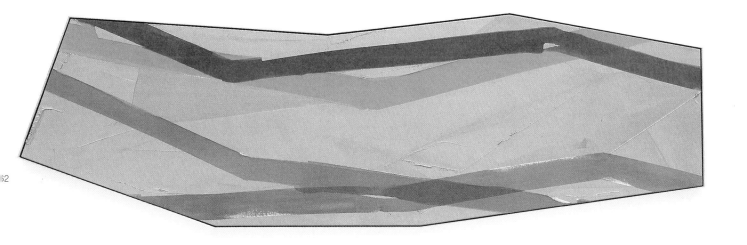

62

62. **Seclude.** 1982.
   Acrylic on canvas, 31 × 105 in. (78.7 × 266.7 cm).
   Collection of the artist.
   Courtesy Salander-O'Reilly Galleries, New York.

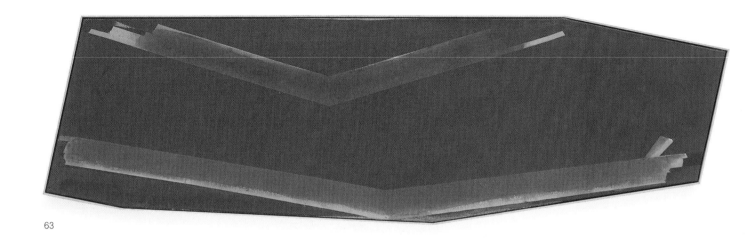

63

63. **Wrap.** 1982.
Acrylic on canvas, 30 × 105 in. (76.2 × 266.7 cm).
Collection of the artist.
Courtesy Salander-O'Reilly Galleries, New York.
Photo: Steven Sloman.

64. **Repeal.** 1982.
Acrylic on canvas, 95⅝ × 43 in. (242.8 × 109.2 cm).
Courtesy Salander-O'Reilly Galleries, New York.

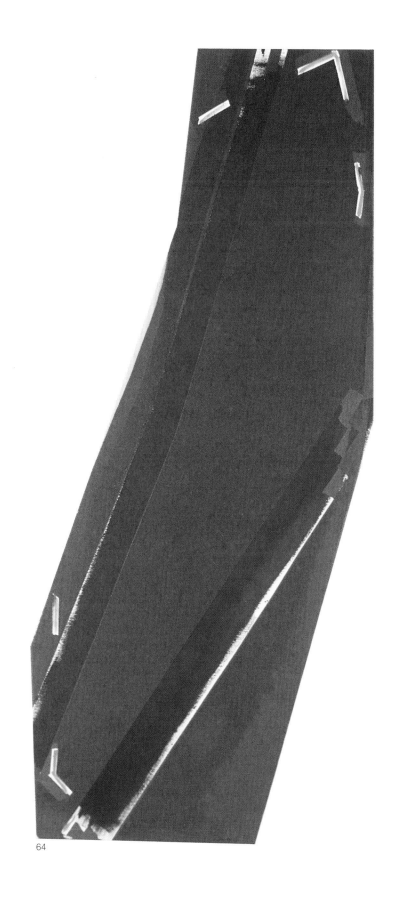

64

65. **Bravo Barcelona.** 1983.
Monotype on Guarro paper, 41 × 29 in. (104 × 74.6 cm).
Courtesy Galeria Joan Prats, Barcelonà.

66. **Green's Vanity.** 1983.
Acrylic on canvas, 84¼ × 119¾ in. (214 × 304 cm).
Private collection.
Courtesy Galerie de France.

67. **Comet.** 1983.
   Acrylic on canvas, 85 × 69½ in. (216 × 176.5 cm).
   Collection of the artist.
   Courtesy Salander-O'Reilly Galleries, New York.

68. **Jazz.** 1983.
Acrylic on canvas, 85 × 69½ in. (216 × 176.5 cm).
Gerald Piltzer Collection.

69. **Periplum.** 1985.
Acrylic on canvas, 87 × 214½ in. (221 × 544.5 cm).
Gaspar Collection.
Courtesy R.H. Love Galleries.

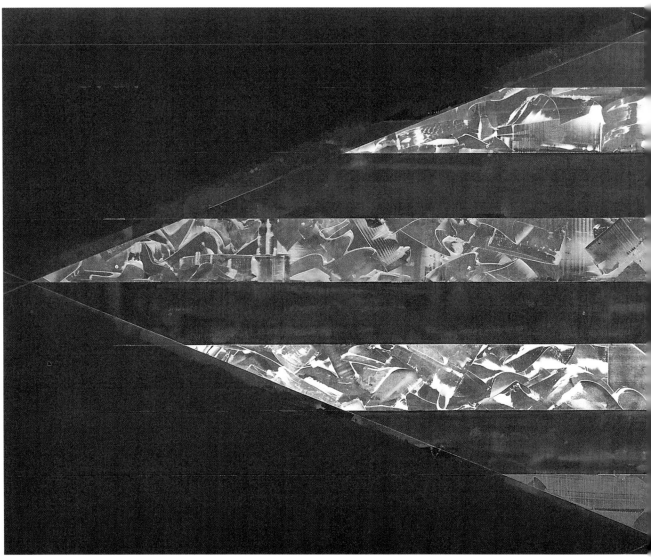

69

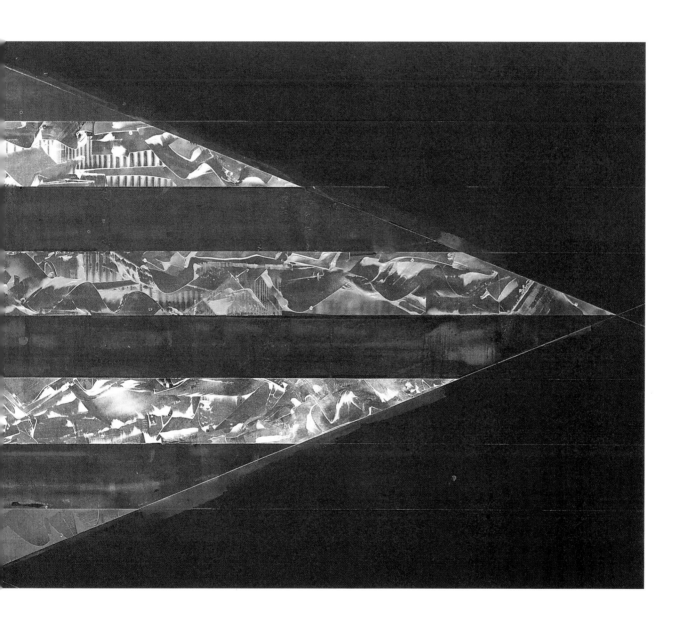

70. **Stardust.** 1985.
  Acrylic on canvas, 89¼ × 89¼ in. (226.7 × 226.7 cm).
  Tochigi Prefectural Museum of Fine Arts.

71. **Highlights.** 1985-1986.
Acrylic on canvas, 101½ × 79 in. (257.8 × 200.6 cm).
Francis J. Greenburger Collection.

72. **AM - PM.** 1986.
   Acrylic on canvas, 78 × 54 in. (198 × 137.1 cm).
   Private collection, Toronto.

73. **Cinch.** 1986.
Acrylic on canvas, 98⅛ × 81⅞ in. (249.2 × 208 cm).
Mr. and Mrs. Eldon C. Mayer, Jr. Collection.
Photo: Steven Sloman.

74. **Steel Reflect.** 1986.
Acrylic on canvas, 66 × 44¾ in. (167.6 × 113.7 cm).
Collection of the artist.
Courtesy Salander-O'Reilly Galleries, New York.

75. **Gift of Reason.** 1986.
    Acrylic on canvas, 66 × 42 in. (167.6 × 106.7 cm).
    Collection of the artist.
    Courtesy Salander-O'Reilly Galleries, New York.
    Photo: Steven Sloman.

76. **Doors: Parisian Bars.** 1987.
Acrylic and Plexiglass on canvas, 19¼ × 20¼ in. (48.9 × 51.5 cm).
Courtesy Salander-O'Reilly Galleries, New York.

76

77. **Thresholds.** 1987.
Acrylic on canvas, 80 × 72¾ in. (203.2 × 184.7 cm).
Private collection.

78. **Flow.** 1987.
Acrylic on canvas mounted on panels, $73 \times 80\frac{3}{4}$ in. (185.5×205 cm).
Collection of the artist.
Courtesy Salander-O'Reilly Galleries, New York.

79. **Shadows.** 1987.
Acrylic on canvas mounted on panels, 80½ × 69 in. (204.5 × 175.2 cm).
Collection of the artist.
Courtesy Salander-O'Reilly Galleries, New York.
Photo: Steven Sloman.

80. **Side Boards.** 1987.
   Acrylic on canvas mounted on panels, 72 × 80¼ in. (183 × 203.2 cm).
   Collection of the artist.
   Courtesy Salander-O'Reilly Galleries, New York.
   Photo: Steven Sloman.

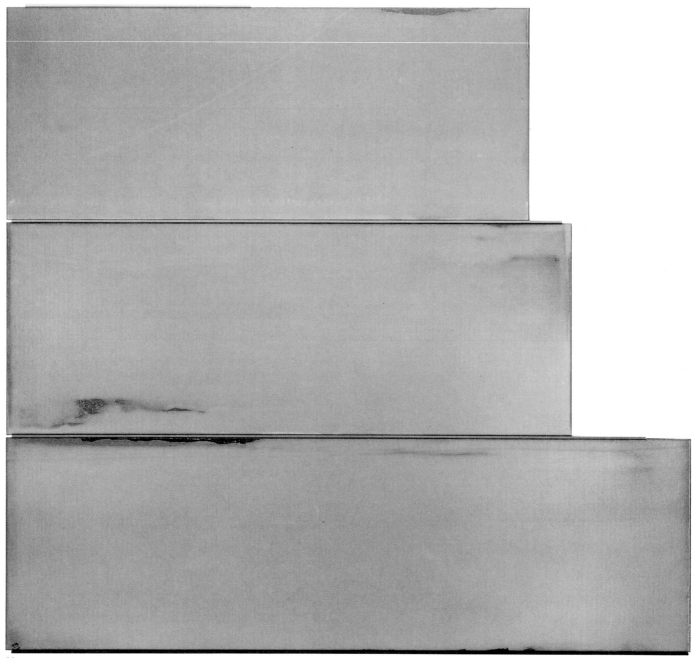

81. **Doors: Step by Step.** 1987.
   Acrylic on canvas mounted on wood with Plexiglass, 88½ × 78½ in. (224.7 × 199.4 cm).
   Collection of the artist.
   Courtesy Salander-O'Reilly Galleries, New York.

82. **Doors: Foreground: Middleground: Background.** 1989.
   Acrylic on canvas mounted on panel with Plexiglass, 74¼×81 in. (188.5×205.7 cm).
   Private collection.

83. **Ignited Dream.** 1988.
   Acrylic on canvas with Plexiglass, 85½ × 55 in. (217.2 × 141 cm).
   Collection of the artist.
   Courtesy Gallery One, Toronto.

84. **Doors: Dark/Sky Blue.** 1988.
Acrylic on canvas, 80 × 37 in. (203.2 × 94 cm).
Collection of the artist.
Courtesy Salander-O'Reilly Galleries, New York.
Photo: Steven Sloman.

85. **Doors: Gold.** 1988.
    Acrylic on canvas mounted on wood, with Plexiglass, 80 × 35½ in. (203 × 90 cm).
    Courtesy the artist.
    Photo: Gamma One Conversions, New York.

86. **Sea View.** 1988.
Acrylic on canvas, 80½ × 49 in. (204.4 × 124.4 cm).
Private collection.

87. **Doors: One O'Clock Jump.** 1989.
Acrylic on canvas mounted on wood, with Plexiglass, 80 × 37¼ in. (203 × 94.5 cm).
Courtesy Salander-O'Reilly Galleries, New York.
Photo: Osamu Nishihira.

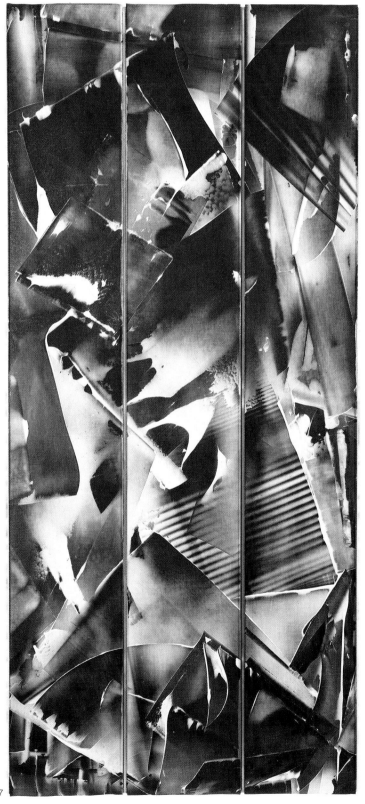

88. **Doors: No Way Through.** 1989.
Acrylic on canvas, 37 × 45 in. (94 × 114.3 cm).
Collection of the artist.
Courtesy Salander-O'Reilly Galleries, New York.
Photo: Steven Sloman.

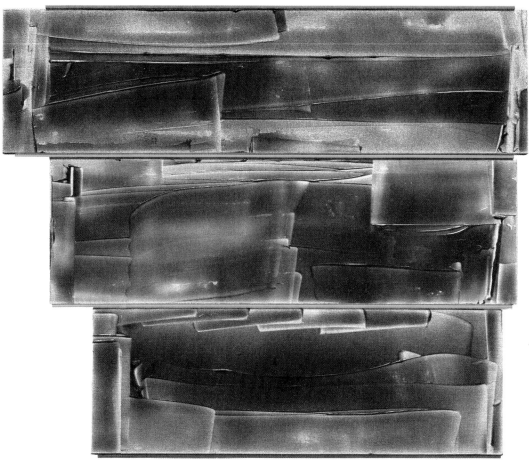

88

89. **Scatter.** 1989.
    Acrylic on canvas mounted on wood, with Plexiglass, 36 × 45 in. (91.5 × 114.3 cm).
    Courtesy the artist.
    Photo: Gamma One Conversions, New York.

89

90. **Doors: Curtain Tempest.** 1990.
Acrylic on canvas mounted on
wood, with Plexiglass,
80 × 25 in. (203 × 63.5 cm).
Courtesy the artist.
Photo: Osamu Nishihira.

91. **Doors: Inside Heat.** 1990.
Acrylic on canvas mounted on
wood, with Plexiglass,
80 × 28¼ in. (203 × 71.7 cm).
Courtesy the artist.
Photo: Gamma One
Conversions, New York.

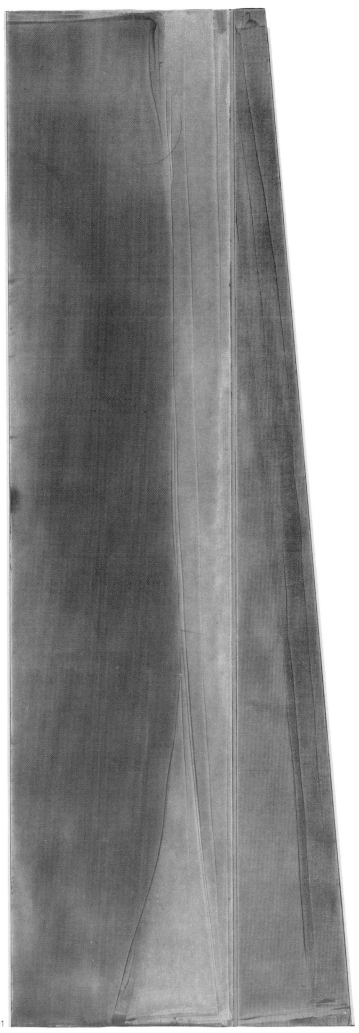

92. **Carpinteria: Arch.** 1990.
Acrylic on canvas mounted on
wood, with Plexiglass,
97¼×26¼ in. (247×66.7 cm).
Courtesy the artist.
Photo: Kevin J. Delahay.

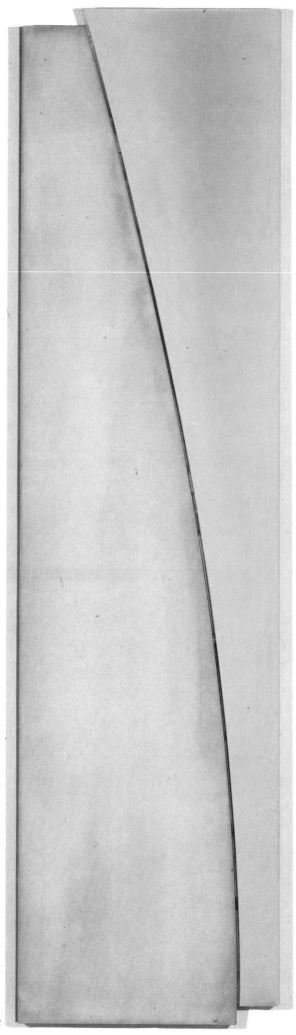

93. **Doors: Night Breeze.** 1990.
Acrylic on canvas on panels, 19³/₈ × 20¹/₈ in. (49 × 51 cm).
Collection of the artist.

93

94

94. **Carpinteria: Dream of Joy.**
    1990.
    Acrylic on canvas mounted on
    wood, with Plexiglass,
    83½ × 40¾ in.
    (212 × 103.5 cm).
    Courtesy the artist.
    Photo: Kevin J. Delahay.

95. **Carpinteria: Flare.** 1990.
    Acrylic on canvas mounted on
    wood, with Plexiglass,
    95½ × 55½ in.
    (242.5 × 141 cm).
    Courtesy the artist.
    Photo: Kevin J. Delahay

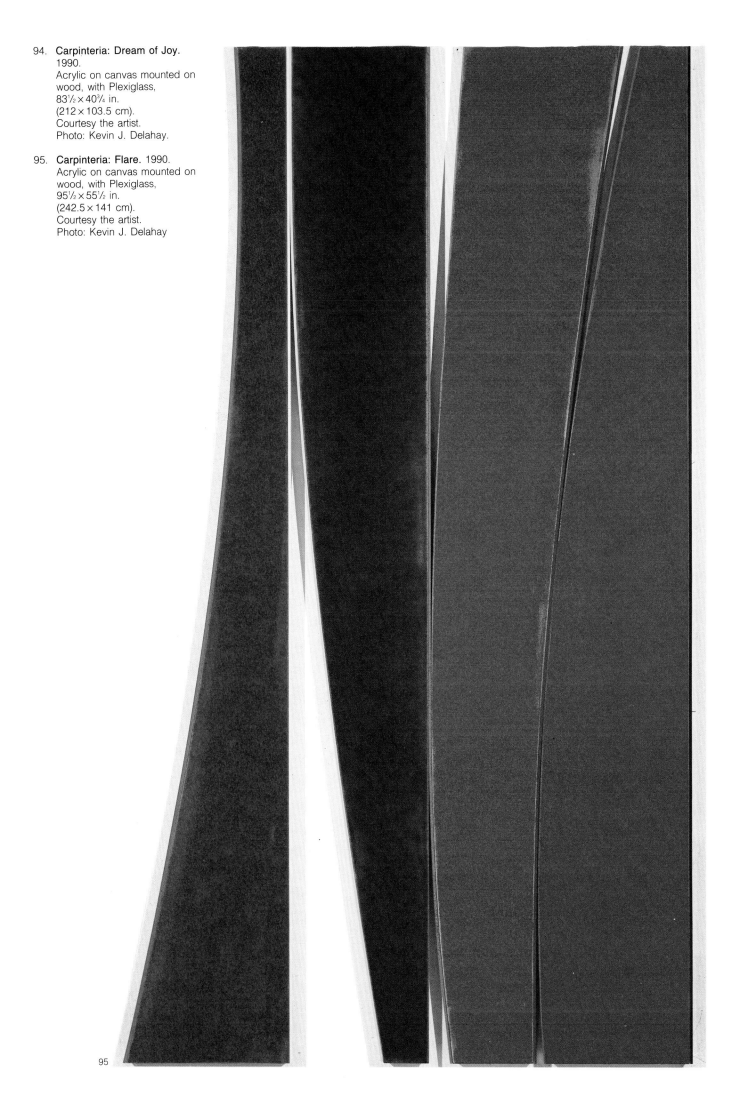

96 and 97. **The Weisner Building.**
  Massachusetts Institute of Technology, Boston, Mass.

LIST OF ILLUSTRATIONS

1. **Luster.** 1958.
Magna on canvas,
59 × 59 in. (149.8 × 149.8 cm).
Private collection.

2. **This.** 1958-1959.
Acrylic on canvas,
84 × 84 in. (213.3 × 213.3 cm).
Courtesy Salander-O'Reilly Galleries,
New York.

3. **That.** 1958-1959.
Acrylic on canvas,
81¾ × 81¾ in. (207.6 × 207.6 cm).
Mr. and Mrs. David Mirvish Collection,
Toronto.

4. **Untitled.** 1959.
Acrylic on canvas,
33¾ × 33¾ in. (85.7 × 85.7 cm).
Courtesy Salander-O'Reilly Galleries,
New York.

5. **Fête.** 1959.
Magna on canvas,
69 × 70 in. (175.2 × 177.8 cm).
Courtesy Salander-O'Reilly Galleries,
New York.

6. **Whirl.** 1960.
Acrylic on canvas,
70¾ × 69½ in. (179.7 × 176.5 cm).
Coffin Fine Arts Trust Fund, 1974;
Nathan Emory Coffin Collection of the
Des Moines Center.

7. **Bloom.** 1960.
Acrylic on canvas,
66⅞ × 67⅛ in. (170 × 171 cm).
Kunstsammlung Nordrhein-Westfalen,
Düsseldorf.

8. **Earthen Bound.** 1960.
Acrylic on canvas,
103¼ × 103¼ in. (262.2 × 262.2 cm).
Collection of the artist.
Courtesy Salander-O'Reilly Galleries,
New York.

9. **The Nightingale.** 1960.
Acrylic on canvas,
68½ × 68½ in. (174 × 174 cm).
Mr. and Mrs. Arthur Rock Collection.

10. **Nieuport.** 1960.
Acrylic on canvas,
68½ × 68½ in. (174 × 174 cm).
Art Gallery of Ontario, Toronto.
Photo: Karol Ike

11. **Flutter.** 1960.
Oil on canvas,
67 × 67¼ in. (170.2 × 170.8 cm).
Steve Martin Collection.

12. **Inner Way.** 1961.
Acrylic on canvas,
83 × 83 in. (210.8 × 210.8 cm).
Mr. and Mrs. Graham Gund Collection,
Cambridge, Mass.

13. **Turnsole.** 1961.
Synthetic polymer paint on canvas,
94⅛ × 94¼ in. (239 × 239 cm).
Collection, The Museum of Modern Art,
New York. Blanchette Rockefeller Fund.

14. **Winter Sun.** 1962.
Acrylic on canvas with Plexiglass,
69¾ × 69½ in. (177 × 176.5 cm).
Emanuel Hoffman-Foundation, Museum
für Gegenwartskunst Basilea.

15. **Matter of Midnight.** 1963.
Acrylic on canvas,
72 × 72 in. (182.8 × 182.8 cm).
Collection of the David Mirvish Gallery,
Toronto.

16. **Dusk.** 1963.
Synthetic polymer on canvas,
94¾ × 76 in. (240.8 × 193.1 cm).
Hirshhorn Museum and Sculpture
Garden Smithsonian Institution.
Gift of Joseph H. Hirshhorn, 1966.

17. **Red, White and Green.** 1963.
Acrylic on canvas,
80¾ × 117⅜ in. (205 × 298 cm).
Courtesy Salander-O'Reilly Galleries,
New York.

18. **Bend Sinister.** 1964.
Synthetic polymer on canvas,
92½ × 162½ in. (235 × 411.5 cm).
Hirshhorn Museum and Sculpture
Garden Smithsonian Institution.
Gift of Joseph H. Hirshhorn, 1966.

19. **And Again.** 1964.
Acrylic on canvas,
69 × 69 in. (175.2 × 175.2 cm).
Mr. and Mrs. Bagley Wright Collection.

20. **C.** 1964.
Acrylic plastic on canvas,
69¾ × 69¾ in. (177.2 × 177.2 cm).
Art Gallery of Ontario, Toronto. Gift from
Corporations Subscription Fund, 1965.
Photo: Carlo Catenazzi.

21. **Blue Plus Eight.** 1964.
Acrylic on canvas,
69½ × 69½ in. (176.5 × 176.5 cm).
Collection of the David Mirvish Gallery,
Toronto.

22. **Plunge.** 1965.
Acrylic on canvas,
48 × 48 in. (122 × 122 cm).
Mrs. Anne Mirvish Collection, Toronto.

23. **No Bid.** 1965.
Acrylic on canvas,
46 × 46 in. (117 × 117 cm).
Private collection, Toronto.

24. **Dark Sweet Cherry.** 1966.
Acrylic on canvas,
60 × 86 in. (152.4 × 218.5 cm).
Collection of the David Mirvish Gallery,
Toronto.

25. **Grave Light.** 1965.
Acrylic on canvas,
102 × 210 in. (259 × 533 cm).
The Gund Art Foundation.

26. **Untitled.** 1965.
Acrylic on canvas,
63½ × 63½ in. (161.2 × 161.2 cm).
Private collection.

27. **Greenbrier.** 1966.
Acrylic on canvas,
24 × 69 in. (61 × 175.2 cm).
Courtesy Salander-O'Reilly Galleries,
New York.

28. **Untitled.** 1966.
Acrylic on canvas,
96 × 24 in. (243.8 × 61 cm).
Private collection.

29. **Must.** 1966.
Acrylic on canvas,
48 × 96 in. (121.9 × 243.8 cm).
Collection of The Edmonton Art Gallery,
Alberta. Donated by Westburne Int. Ind.

30. **Jump.** 1966.
Acrylic on canvas,
35 × 120 in. (88.9 × 305 cm).
Collection of the David Mirvish Gallery,
Toronto.

31. **Shade.** 1966.
Acrylic on canvas,
24 × 96 in. (61 × 243.8 cm).
Mr. and Mrs. David Mirvish Collection,
Toronto.

32. **Approach.** 1966.
Acrylic on canvas,
96 × 22 in. (243.8 × 56 cm).
Private collection.

33. **Pause.** 1966.
Acrylic on canvas,
36 × 102 in. (91.4 × 259.1 cm).
Private collection.
Photo: Mick Hales.

34. **In the Curl.** 1967.
Acrylic on canvas,
96 × 24 in. (243.8 × 61 cm).
Courtesy Salander-O'Reilly Galleries,
New York.

35. **Magus.** 1967.
Acrylic on canvas,
86½ × 270 in. (219.7 × 685.5 cm).
Collection of the David Mirvish Gallery,
Toronto.

36. **Via Token.** 1969.
Acrylic on canvas,
100¼ × 240 in. (254.6 × 610 cm).
Collection of the David Mirvish Gallery,
Toronto.

37. **Via Tradewind.** 1968.
Acrylic on canvas,
53 × 114 in. (134.6 × 289.5 cm).
Dr. and Mrs. Paul Tunick Collection,
New York.
Photo: Silvia Sarner.

38. **Mexican Camino.** 1970.
Acrylic on canvas,
164 × 44 in. (416.5 × 111.7 cm).
Mr. and Mrs. Harry W. Anderson
Collection, Atherton, Ca.

39. **Brief Rhythm.** 1971.
Acrylic on canvas,
58½ × 56⅛ in. (148.5 × 142.5 cm).
Courtesy Salander-O'Reilly Galleries,
New York.

40. **Sutters Mill.** 1971.
Acrylic on canvas,
91³/₄ × 31¹/₂ in. (233 × 80 cm).
Mr. and Mrs. Michael Steiner Collection.

41. **Circum Grid Green.** 1973.
Acrylic on canvas,
79 in. (200.6 cm) diameter.
Collection of the David Mirvish Gallery,
Toronto.

42. **Paralax.** 1973.
Acrylic on canvas,
79 in. (200.6 cm) diameter.
Collection of the David Mirvish Gallery,
Toronto.

43. **Reigning Rule.** 1973.
Acrylic on canvas,
74¹/₄ × 74¹/₄ in. (188.5 × 188.5 cm).
Collection of the David Mirvish Gallery,
Toronto.

44. **Burnt Beige.** 1975.
Acrylic on canvas,
112 × 95¹/₂ in. (284.5 × 242.5 cm).
Leo Castelli, New York.

45. **Ova Ray.** 1976.
Acrylic on canvas,
85 × 106³/₄ in. (215.8 × 271 cm).
Collection of the artist.
Courtesy Salander-O'Reilly Galleries,
New York.
Photo: Steven Sloman.

46. **Moon Ray.** 1976.
Acrylic on canvas,
63¹/₄ × 84³/₄ in. (160.6 × 215.2 cm).
Collection of the artist.
Courtesy Salander-O'Reilly Galleries,
New York.
Photo: Steven Sloman.

47. **Field of Green.** 1977.
Acrylic on canvas,
65¹/₂ × 98¹/₂ in. (166.3 × 250 cm).
Courtesy Salander-O'Reilly Galleries,
New York.

48. **C and H.** 1977.
Acrylic on canvas,
60 × 90 in. (152.3 × 228.5 cm).
Collection of the artist.
Courtesy Salander-O'Reilly Galleries,
New York.
Photo: Steven Sloman.

49. **Turns.** 1977.
Acrylic on canvas,
69³/₄ × 94³/₄ in. (177 × 240.6 cm).
Courtesy Salander-O'Reilly Galleries,
New York.

50. **Rejoin.** 1980.
Acrylic on canvas,
74¹/₂ × 162¹/₂ in. (189 × 412.5 cm).
Collection of the artist.
Courtesy Salander-O'Reilly Galleries,
New York.
Photo: Steven Sloman.

51. **Sweet Box.** 1978.
Acrylic on canvas,
61 × 71 in. (155 × 180.3 cm).
Private collection, Sioux City, Iowa.

52. **Adjoin.** 1980.
Acrylic on canvas,
88¹/₂ × 178³/₄ in. (224.7 × 454 cm),
irregular.
Mr. and Mrs. Graham Gund Collection.
Photo: Greg Heins.

53. **Occurent.** 1979.
Acrylic on canvas,
36³/₄ × 114¹/₄ in. (93.3 × 290.2 cm).
Collection of the artist.
Courtesy Salander-O'Reilly Galleries,
New York.
Photo: Steven Sloman.

54. **Vessel.** 1980.
Acrylic on canvas,
79¹/₂ × 166 in. (202 × 421.6 cm).
Private collection.
Photo: Steve Sloman.

55. **Second.** 1979.
Acrylic on canvas,
39³/₈ × 107³/₄ in. (100 × 273.7 cm).
A. J. Pyrch Collection, Victoria B.C.

56. **Silver.** 1980.
Acrylic on canvas,
95¹/₂ × 19¹/₈ in. (242.5 × 48.6 cm).
Roger Diener Collection, Basel.

57. **Flare.** 1981.
Acrylic on canvas,
22 × 92 in. (55.9 × 233.7 cm).
Dr. and Mrs. Everett Ref Collection.

58. **Apace.** 1981.
Acrylic on canvas,
79¹/₂ × 32¹/₂ in. (202 × 82.5 cm).
Lisa Dennison Collection.

59. **Begin and End.** 1981.
Acrylic on canvas,
19³/₈ × 96¹/₂ in. (49 × 245 cm).
Collection of the artist.
Courtesy Salander-O'Reilly Galleries,
New York.
Photo: Steven Sloman.

60. **Reppearance.** 1981.
Acrylic on canvas,
17¹/₂ × 99 in. (44.5 × 251.5 cm).
Courtesy Salander-O'Reilly Galleries,
New York.

61. **Silver Shade.** 1982.
Acrylic on canvas,
17 × 81 in. (43.2 × 205.7 cm).
Collection of the artist.
Courtesy Salander-O'Reilly Galleries,
New York.
Photo: Steven Sloman.

62. **Seclude.** 1982.
Acrylic on canvas,
31 × 105 in. (78.7 × 266.7 cm).
Collection of the artist.
Courtesy Salander-O'Reilly Galleries,
New York.

63. **Wrap.** 1982.
Acrylic on canvas,
30 × 105 in. (76.2 × 266.7 cm).
Collection of the artist.
Courtesy Salander-O'Reilly Galleries,
New York.
Photo: Steven Sloman.

64. **Repeal.** 1982.
Acrylic on canvas,
95⁵/₈ × 43 in. (242.8 × 109.2 cm).
Courtesy Salander-O'Reilly Galleries,
New York.

65. **Bravo Barcelona.** 1983.
Monotype on Guarro paper,
41 × 29 in. (104 × 74.6 cm).
Courtesy Galeria Joan Prats, Barcelona.

66. **Green's Vanity.** 1983.
Acrylic on canvas,
84¹/₄ × 119³/₄ in. (214 × 304 cm).
Private collection.
Courtesy Galerie de France.

67. **Comet.** 1983.
Acrylic on canvas,
85 × 69¹/₂ in. (216 × 176.5 cm).
Collection of the artist.
Courtesy Salander-O'Reilly Galleries,
New York.

68. **Jazz.** 1983.
Acrylic on canvas,
85 × 69¹/₂ in. (216 × 176.5 cm).
Gerald Piltzer Collection.

69. **Periplum.** 1985.
Acrylic on canvas,
87 × 214¹/₂ in. (221 × 544.5 cm).
Gaspar Collection.
Courtesy R.H. Love Galleries.

70. **Stardust.** 1985.
Acrylic on canvas,
89¹/₄ × 89¹/₄ in. (226.7 × 226.7 cm).
Tochigi Prefectural Museum of Fine
Arts.

71. **Highlights.** 1985-1986.
Acrylic on canvas,
101¹/₂ × 79 in. (257.8 × 200.6 cm).
Francis J. Greenburger Collection.

72. **AM - PM.** 1986.
Acrylic on canvas,
78 × 54 in. (198 × 137.1 cm).
Private collection, Toronto.

73. **Cinch.** 1986.
Acrylic on canvas,
98¹/₈ × 81⁷/₈ in. (249.2 × 208 cm).
Mr. and Mrs. Eldon C. Mayer, Jr.
Collection.
Photo: Steven Sloman.

74. **Steel Reflect.** 1986.
Acrylic on canvas,
66 × 44³/₄ in. (167.6 × 113.7 cm).
Collection of the artist.
Courtesy Salander-O'Reilly Galleries,
New York.

75. **Gift of Reason.** 1986.
Acrylic on canvas,
66 × 42 in. (167.6 × 106.7 cm).
Collection of the artist.
Courtesy Salander-O'Reilly Galleries,
New York.
Photo: Steven Sloman.

76. **Doors: Parisian Bars.** 1987.
Acrylic and Plexiglass on canvas,
19¹/₄ × 20¹/₄ in. (48.9 × 51.5 cm).
Courtesy Salander-O'Reilly Galleries,
New York.

77. **Thresholds.** 1987.
Acrylic on canvas,
80 × 72¾ in. (203.2 × 184.7 cm).
Private collection.

78. **Flow.** 1987.
Acrylic on canvas mounted on panels,
73 × 80¾ in. (185.5 × 205 cm).
Collection of the artist.
Courtesy Salander-O'Reilly Galleries,
New York.

79. **Shadows.** 1987.
Acrylic on canvas mounted on panels,
80½ × 69 in. (204.5 × 175.2 cm).
Collection of the artist.
Courtesy Salander-O'Reilly Galleries,
New York.
Photo: Steven Sloman.

80. **Side Boards.** 1987.
Acrylic on canvas mounted on panels,
72 × 80¼ in. (183 × 203.2 cm).
Collection of the artist.
Courtesy Salander-O'Reilly Galleries,
New York.
Photo: Steven Sloman.

81. **Doors: Step by Step.** 1987.
Acrylic on canvas mounted on wood
with Plexiglass,
88½ × 78½ in. (224.7 × 199.4 cm).
Collection of the artist.
Courtesy Salander-O'Reilly Galleries,
New York.

82. **Doors: Foreground: Middleground:
Background.** 1989.
Acrylic on canvas mounted on panel
with Plexiglass,
74¼ × 81 in. (188.5 × 205.7 cm).
Private collection.

83. **Ignited Dream.** 1988.
Acrylic on canvas with Plexiglass,
85½ × 55 in. (217.2 × 141 cm).
Collection of the artist.
Courtesy Gallery One, Toronto.

84. **Doors: Dark/Sky Blue.** 1988.
Acrylic on canvas,
80 × 37 in. (203.2 × 94 cm).
Collection of the artist.
Courtesy Salander-O'Reilly Galleries,
New York.
Photo: Steven Sloman.

85. **Doors: Gold.** 1988.
Acrylic on canvas mounted on wood,
with Plexiglass,
80 × 35½ in. (203 × 90 cm).
Courtesy the artist.
Photo: Gamma One Conversions,
New York.

86. **Sea View.** 1988.
Acrylic on canvas,
80½ × 49 in. (204.4 × 124.4 cm).
Private collection.

87. **Doors: One O'Clock Jump.** 1989.
Acrylic on canvas mounted on wood,
with Plexiglass,
80 × 37¼ in. (203 × 94.5 cm).
Courtesy Salander-O'Reilly Galleries,
New York.
Photo: Osamu Nishihira.

88. **Doors: No Way Through.** 1989.
Acrylic on canvas,
37 × 45 in. (94 × 114.3 cm).
Collection of the artist.
Courtesy Salander-O'Reilly Galleries,
New York.
Photo: Steven Sloman.

89. **Scatter.** 1989.
Acrylic on canvas mounted on wood,
with Plexiglass,
36 × 45 in. (91.5 × 114.3 cm).
Courtesy the artist.
Photo: Gamma One Conversions,
New York.

90. **Doors: Curtain Tempest.** 1990.
Acrylic on canvas mounted on wood,
with Plexiglass,
80 × 25 in. (203 × 63.5 cm).
Courtesy the artist.
Photo: Osamu Nishihira.

91. **Doors: Inside Heat.** 1990.
Acrylic on canvas mounted on wood,
with Plexiglass,
80 × 28¼ in. (203 × 71.7 cm).
Courtesy the artist.
Photo: Gamma Oner Conversions,
New York.

92. **Carpinteria: Arch.** 1990.
Acrylic on canvas mounted on wood,
with Plexiglass,
97¼ × 26¼ in. (247 × 66.7 cm).
Courtesy the artist.
Photo: Kevin J. Delahay.

93. **Doors: Night Breeze.** 1990.
Acrylic on canvas on panels,
19⅜ × 20⅛ in. (49 × 51 cm).
Collection of the artist.

94. **Carpinteria: Dream of Joy.** 1990.
Acrylic on canvas mounted on wood,
with Plexiglass,
83½ × 40¾ in. (212 × 103.5 cm).
Courtesy the artist.
Photo: Kevin J. Delahay.

95. **Carpinteria: Flare.** 1990.
Acrylic on canvas mounted on wood,
with Plexiglass,
95½ × 55½ in. (242.5 × 141 cm).
Courtesy the artist.
Photo: Kevin J. Delahay

96 and 97. **The Weisner Building.**
Massachusetts Institute of Technology,
Boston, Mass.